Paul Robeson

PAUL ROBESON

*Hero
Before His
Time*

*Rebecca
Larsen*

Franklin Watts
New York London Toronto Sydney
(1989)

Photographs courtesy of:
Movie Star News: p. 2; Rutgers University: pp. 99, 100;
UPI/Bettmann Newsphotos: pp. 101, 102 (both), 103, 104,
105, 106, 107, 108, 109, 110, 112; Sovfoto: p. 111.

Library of Congress Cataloging-in-Publication Data

Larsen, Rebecca.
Paul Robeson, hero before his time / by Rebecca Larsen.
p.   cm.
Bibliography: p.
Includes index
Summary: Surveys the personal life and career of the singer,
actor, and political activist.
ISBN 0-531-15117-4. — ISBN 0-531-10779-5 (lib. bdg.)
1. Robeson, Paul, 1898-1976—Juvenile literature.   2. Afro-
Americans—Biography—Juvenile literature.   3. Actors—United
States—Biography—Juvenile literature.   4. Singers—United States—
Biography—Juvenile literature.   [1. Robeson, Paul, 1898-1976.
2. Actors and actresses.   3. Singers.   4. Afro-Americans—
Biography.]   I. Title.
E185.97.R63L37   1989
782'.0092—DC20
[B]   [92]   89-8880   CIP   AC

Contents

Paul Robeson

"An abiding sense of comfort and security"

The 1890s, when Paul Robeson was born, marked a harsh, difficult era for blacks in the United States. Less than forty years before, the Civil War had ended and the nation had freed its slaves.

But freedom did not bring equality. In the 1890s, lynch mobs murdered more than a hundred blacks each year. Although blacks had the right to vote, election fraud in the South reduced their power at the ballot box. Just before Paul Robeson was born, the Supreme Court upheld a Louisiana law that said railroads must provide separate seats and restrooms for blacks. Supposedly, these so-called Jim Crow facilities were separate but equal. In reality, they were dirty and shabby imitations of what whites used.

Paul Robeson was born far away from the troubled South in Princeton, New Jersey, a quiet well-educated community fifty miles from New York. But blacks and whites there were still sharply divided, partly because so many students and faculty at prestigious Princeton University came from the Deep South. Princeton public schools were segregated, and for many years no blacks could go to the university. It was like living on a Southern plantation, Paul Robeson said. "And with no more dignity than that suggests—the bowing and scraping to the drunken rich, all the vile names, all the Uncle Tomming to earn enough to lead miserable lives."[1]

Blacks had modest homes in west Princeton. "The people of our small Negro community were, for the most part, a servant class," Paul Robeson said, "domestics in the homes of the wealthy, serving as cooks, waiters and caretakers at the university, coachmen for the town and laborers at the nearby farms and brickyards."[2]

Paul's father, William Drew Robeson, was a highly respected pastor who took courageous stands on behalf of his black congregation. His powerful, melodic voice added to his reputation as an orator. He was college educated in an era when few Americans even graduated from high school, and he was broad-shouldered and dignified looking. "From him we learned, and never doubted it, that the Negro was in every way the equal of the white man," Paul Robeson said.[3]

The Reverend Robeson had been born to a slave couple, in a one-room cabin on a North Carolina plantation. The name "Robeson" probably was taken from the white family who owned William Robeson. But in 1860, just before the Civil War, William Robeson fled North via the Underground Railroad that helped slaves escape. After serving in the Union Army, he worked his way through the Presbyterian divinity school at the all-black Lincoln University near Philadelphia.

At thirty-three, the Reverend Robeson married Maria Louisa Bustill, a quiet, devout twenty-five-year-old schoolteacher, who belonged to a Philadelphia family of scholars, artists, and teachers with Indian and Quaker ancestors. Maria Louisa's great-grandfather, Cyrus, had even baked bread for George Washington's starving troops at Valley Forge.

During the first twenty years of their marriage, William and Maria Bustill had eight children, of whom five survived. On April 9, 1898, they had their last baby, a large and healthy son, named Paul Leroy Robeson. Baby Paul was born in the parsonage on Witherspoon Street where the Reverend Robeson had been preaching in a Presbyterian church for more than two decades. Paul had three older brothers and a sister: William D., Jr., Reeve (sometimes called Reed), Benjamin, and Marion.

Tragedy split this tightly knit family when Paul was just six years old. By then, Paul's mother, Maria Louisa Bustill, was over fifty and wore thick glasses for eye problems. Asthma also troubled her breathing. But even so, one January morning in 1904, she decided to give her house a thorough cleaning. Her husband was away on business, and four of her children, including Paul, were at school. But Benjamin, twelve, had stayed home to help his mother.

Mrs. Robeson began lifting the parlor stove while Ben pulled away the carpet. As she worked, a hot coal fell out and set fire to her dress. As she beat with her hands at the flames in her full skirts, Ben ran screaming out of the house to fetch a neighbor who doused the fire.

A doctor summoned by Ben used quarts of linseed oil and limewater on Maria Louisa's badly burned feet, legs, and hands. But her life ebbed away in a few last painful hours. The friends and relatives at her bed were amazed at the courage of this woman known for the aid she gave to the sick, poor, and orphans. She said farewell to her husband and recited the First and Twenty-Third psalms over and over again. "This is the way I am to go," she told them, "and because God intended it I am content."[4]

For young Paul, that dark day erased many memories of his mother: "I remember her lying in the coffin, and the funeral, and the relatives who came, but it must be that the pain and shock of her death blotted out all other personal recollections."[5]

More than ever Paul focused on his father, now sixty. "I loved him like no one in all the world," he said.[6] Once when he proudly brought home a report card with six A's and one B in Latin, his father questioned him about the B. Paul defended himself: "I'm at the head of the class, and the other fellows are thankful if they get two or three A's."

"We'll have to put a little more time on Caesar next month, and see if we can't get an A in that too," his father replied.[7]

But there were also winter evenings of checkers when Paul and his father played for hours in the parlor, games of football on a weed-grown lot with brother Bill, by then a Lincoln University student, and sessions of Follow the Leader and Run Sheep Run with neighbor children, some of them white. "There must have been moments when I felt the sorrows of a motherless child, but what I most remember from my youngest days was an abiding sense of comfort and security," Paul Robeson said.[8]

Always their music surrounded Paul, on the back porches, in the parlors and in church: hymns and ragtime, gospel and blues, and always black spirituals. Even his father's sermons had the phrasing and rhythm of folk songs, Paul Robeson said.

Many relatives, including Paul's father, sensed something special about Paul and told him he would have a great future. "Somehow they were sure of it, and because of that belief they added an extra measure to the affection they lavished on their preacher's motherless child," Paul Robeson later remembered.[9]

A cloud of financial trouble hung over those years as well. When Paul was eight years old, his father had been removed from the pulpit of his Princeton church due to a dispute among the church members, including some of his relatives. The Reverend Robeson had to move out of the church parsonage and find a new way to make a living. With a wagon and a horse named Bess, he began to haul ashes for the townsfolk to dump them in his backyard. He also served as a coachman for students. But to Paul "he was still the dignified Reverend Robeson to the community, and no man carried himself with greater pride."[10]

In 1907, the Reverend Robeson moved thirty miles away to Westfield. At first he worked in a grocery store and lived with Paul and Ben in an attic over the store. Although William Robeson was already 62, a time when many people want to retire, he decided to start a church in a different denomination, the African Methodist Episcopal Zion Church. Westfield's black community was small, and he began with only about a dozen members in his church on Downing Street.

For Paul, Westfield meant a new lifestyle, attending school with white children and making friends among whites and blacks. "I was popular with the other boys and girls because of my skill at sports and studies, and because I was always ready to share in their larks and fun-making."[11] White parents also found the preacher's son a good example for their children because of his report card, his respect for elders, and the fact that he never smoked or missed church.

Soon Paul and his father moved to Somerville, New Jersey, where the Reverend Robeson became pastor of another church. Paul's father's reputation grew because of his affectionate, generous personality, the same qualities that many said Paul had as an adult. When the Reverend Robeson walked down the main street of tiny Somerville, a few blocks took hours as friends and congregation members insisted that he stop to chat.

"Don't you ever take it, as long as you live"

During the years when Paul Robeson was growing up, America's blacks were torn by different philosophies about how they could improve their economic and political lot. On the one hand, they lived in the shadow of Booker T. Washington, the self-educated, former slave and leader of Tuskegee Institute. Whites admired his determination and hard work. But to many, Washington was someone who believed blacks must move slowly in seeking their rights. "I believe it is the duty of the Negro . . . to deport himself modestly in regard to political claims," Washington wrote.[1] At Tuskegee he urged blacks to study industrial arts, leading many to fear that blacks would always be limited to factory jobs and hard labor.

In contrast, W. E. B. Du Bois, the black educator, writer, and sociologist, argued strongly against limiting blacks in school or any area of life. "Education must not simply teach work," Du Bois argued, "it must teach life."[2] Du Bois, an early forerunner of the black militancy that gave birth to the civil rights movement in the 1960s, helped found the National Association for the Advancement of Colored People in 1909 while Paul Robeson was still in grade school.

Paul's education at largely white Somerville High

School reflected a turning-away from the ideas of Washington. In fact, in high school and college, Paul often read articles and books by Du Bois. "We spoke of Dr. Du Bois as Our Professor, The Doctor, The Dean," Paul later wrote.[3]

His high school English teacher, Anna Miller, encouraged Paul in speaking and debating and featured him in his first production of the Shakespeare play, *Othello*. "Nervous and scared, I struggled through the lines on that solemn occasion . . . and no one in the world could have convinced me then that I should ever try acting again," Paul said.[4]

Most of the white teachers and students welcomed Paul to the glee club and the high school football, basketball, baseball, and track teams. In fact, one chemistry teacher urged Paul to attend the school's parties and dances. But although Paul visited some white students in their homes and made friends with their families, he avoided parties where the only girls to dance with were white. He felt strongly then that no matter how well a black person might fit in with whites in school or on the job, he could not mix with whites socially.

It was tough to be black and smart in a nearly all-white school. "Even while demonstrating that he is really an equal (and, strangely, the proof must be *superior* performance!) the Negro must never appear to be challenging white superiority. Climb up if you can—but don't act 'uppity,' " he later wrote.[5]

Brilliant student or not, Paul was often late to his first class of the morning, largely because he stayed up late at night, and his principal was quick to catch Paul when he was tardy. Reverend Robeson had often given teachers and principals permission to hit or spank Paul, but this time Paul announced angrily: "I don't care what *you* do to me, but if that hateful old principal ever lays a hand on me, I swear I'll try my best to break his neck!"[6]

That fiery temper that flashed out again and again in

Paul's life was also seen in his brother Reed (or Reeve), who worked as a coachman. Paul deeply admired this older brother who carried a bag of small rocks with him to throw at those who offended him with racial insults. Reed was quick to jump off his coachman's seat and beat up gentlemen-students, even though it often landed him in jail. "He never said it," Paul Robeson said, "but he told me day after day: 'Listen to me, kid. Don't you ever take it, as long as you live.' "[7]

Eventually though, Reverend Robeson grew tired of bailing Reed out of jail and asked Reed to leave home. Reed had disappointed his father who expected so much from his children.

But Paul Robeson always remembered his brother with love and respect. His rebelliousness, Robeson said, taught Paul to stand up for his rights. Someday when the majority of blacks have learned how to do so, then life will finally be different for everyone, Paul Robeson contended.

Paul's brother Bill also struggled to cope with the outside world, but in a different way. Bill was an intellectual who studied at several colleges. His bouts of schooling were mixed with times when he had to scramble for money as a Pullman porter or as a redcap at Grand Central Station in New York City.

After years of inching through classes, he earned a degree in medicine, but he could never actually build a practice. His restless mind kept flitting from one intriguing question to another. He should have been a researcher in a laboratory, Paul said, but few jobs like that were then open to blacks. When Bill was at home, he tutored Paul and taught him how to study. Just getting the right answer wasn't enough for Bill. "Yes but *why?*" he would insist sharply.[8]

Bill was also the first to recognize musical talent in Paul. One steamy July afternoon, the Robeson family gathered to sing—everything from "Down by the Old Mill Stream" to Christmas carols. The little chorus tried to hit a minor chord and came out sounding like musical chaos. But amid the noise Bill yelled, "Wait a minute, hit that note again, Paul," and when he did, Bill announced: "Paul, you can sing."[9]

As Paul grew older, he served as Sunday school superintendent in his father's church and also helped lead singing with his as yet untrained but talented voice.

As Paul neared the end of high school, his family assumed he would go to Lincoln University like his father and brother had. But then, the family learned of a special scholarship offered to students in New Jersey at Rutgers College in New Brunswick. Rutgers, about fifteen miles away, was then a small private school where only one or two blacks had previously been admitted.

Paul's father, still short of money, was anxious for him to try for the award although there was a problem. Paul had not taken an earlier preliminary exam for juniors that covered subjects from the first three years of high school. Instead, he would be tested on four years of school in the same three hours that other students were tested on only their senior year. Paul hit the books, often until late at night. Ben, Marion, and Bill tutored him, and Reverend Robeson remained quietly confident that Paul would win. His teachers and classmates wished him well; only his principal, Dr. Ackerman, doubted he could win.

Paul won the scholarship and viewed his victory as a turning point in his life. It wasn't that he wanted to go to Rutgers that badly, because he almost believed he'd be happier at Lincoln. "Deep in my heart from that day on was a conviction which none of the Ackermans of America would ever be able to shake," he said. "Equality might be denied, but I knew I was not inferior."[10]

Suddenly, after a lifetime amid a close and loving family that expected him to succeed, Paul Robeson found himself at all-white, competitive Rutgers, a world where some students clearly hoped he would fail. In his Latin, Greek, physics, math, and history classes, Robeson carried the feeling of responsibility that his father had given him. He had to do well; he represented all blacks.

By his junior year, he was elected to the honor society, Phi Beta Kappa. He was a debating champion and joined the glee club. He was also chosen for Cap and Skull, a senior fraternity of four men, who stood for the best ideals of Rutgers.

But for many of his classmates, Robeson would be best remembered as a football player. Football was played differently in those World War I–era years. Players wore thin leather helmets that looked something like the cap of a barnstorming pilot of that day. Skimpy jerseys and knicker-style pants were stretched over minimal padding. On their feet, players laced up high-top leather shoes. The lack of protective clothing didn't mean that the blocks and tackles weren't tough.

Before freshman Paul Robeson showed up for his first practice, Coach George Foster Sanford, who had heard of Robeson's athletic ability, told the rest of the team that a black was coming out for football. At least half the thirty-man squad threatened to quit rather than play with a black, but after losing to the Princeton team, they were desperate for fresh talent and agreed Robeson could try out for defensive end.

In his first scrimmage, several players decided to put Robeson in his place. Play after play was rigged against him. One player slugged him in the face, breaking his nose, an injury that troubled him as a singer for the rest of his life. Then he was knocked down and another player smashed Robeson's right shoulder with his knee.

Even though Robeson had spent his youth dreaming of a college education, even though he knew his father was expecting him to be a success at Rutgers, the battered seventeen-year-old was ready to quit college and football. That night Robeson's brother Bill came to visit. "Kid, I know what it is," Bill said. "I went through it at Pennsylvania. If you want to quit school go ahead, but I wouldn't like to think, and our father wouldn't like to think, that our family had a quitter."[11]

After ten days in bed and a few more days of rest, Robeson returned to the field. But once again, players seemed to be trying to hurt him. Finally, he made a tackle and was lying down with his right palm on the ground. Another player came along and stepped down hard on his hand. No bones cracked, but the player's cleats ripped off Robeson's fingernails. Hungry for revenge, Robeson jumped to his feet.

The whole first-string backfield rushed at Robeson, and he stretched out his arms and pushed three men down at once. Suddenly, he grabbed the ball carrier, Kelly. "I wanted to kill him, and I meant to kill him," Robeson said of that moment. "It wasn't a thought, it was just a feeling, to kill. I got Kelly in my two hands and I got him up over my head like this. I was going to smash him so hard to the ground that I'd break him right in two."[12]

Just then, Coach Sanford yelled through his megaphone: "Robeson, you're on the varsity." Somehow that stopped Robeson, and suddenly everything was all right, he was accepted as part of the team. Many players became his friends, and they joked about those first brutal practice sessions.

By his junior year, Robeson was making headline after headline in the New York sports pages. Twice he was named to the All-American football team. There were still some incidents of racism involving other teams, particularly those from Southern states. But the victories and the praise of reporters, fellow players, and classmates wiped away some of the hurt and pain. Robeson swept up other honors, earning letters as the catcher on the Rutgers baseball team and center on the basketball team. In track he did discus, javelin, shot-put, and pentathlon.

As a student, Robeson was only beginning to develop his ideas about blacks and discrimination in America. When he graduated as valedictorian of his class, he gave a speech that argued that blacks could succeed if they only tried hard enough. The title of his speech was "The New Idealism," and like many graduation speeches, it revealed a faith that a lone individual can fight on to victory no matter what the obstacles.

"And we are struggling on," he told the audience, "attempting to show that knowledge can be obtained under difficulties; that poverty may give place to affluence; that obscurity is not an absolute bar to distinction, and that a way is open to welfare and happiness to all who will follow the way with resolution and wisdom; that neither the old-time slavery, nor continued prejudice need extinguish self-respect, crush manly ambition or paralyze effort; that no power outside of himself can prevent man from sustaining an honorable character and a useful relation to his day and generation."[13]

It was a moment of triumph. Robeson stood at the head of his class. He had surpassed many whites to achieve great honors and had proven the theme of his speech, that a talented individual making a determined effort can get past any roadblock, regardless of discrimination and prejudice.

Sorrow was mixed with his joy though. The year before, his father, his most ardent admirer and a great source of inspiration, had died. The one person who had cared most for him was gone.

But as he gave his commencement speech, Paul Robeson must have been proud to know that he had fulfilled so many of his father's dreams.

"Dragged into rehearsal"

After graduation, Robeson was on his own with no parent to advise him on his choices. He decided on a career in the law and moved to New York City to live in Harlem and enter the Columbia University Law School.

His choice of Harlem was a natural one, according to a biography written some years later by his future wife, Es-landa. There he found many old friends from college and from New Jersey who were working or studying in New York. Blacks in Harlem knew about his football achievements from reading about him in the newspapers, and he quickly became something of a celebrity on the streets of Harlem. His ability to dance and sing made him popular at parties; his love for sports made him a frequent referee at basketball games for younger players. He willingly sang in church choirs.

To help pay for law school, Robeson played professional football on weekends. Later, from 1934–46, blacks were barred from professional football teams, but at the time that Robeson joined the Akron Pros, the team even had a black coach, Frederick Douglass (Fritz) Pollard. Pollard also coached the Milwaukee Badgers for a while and took Robeson with him to that team, too.

Black players made friends with their teammates, but

life off the field was not easy, and fans made it hard on black players. "Akron was a factory town, and they had some prejudiced people there," Fritz Pollard said. "I had to get dressed for the games in a cigar factory, and they'd send a car over for me before the game. The fans booed me and called me all kinds of names because they had a lot of Southerners up there working. I couldn't eat in the restaurants or stay in the hotels."[1]

In spite of these pressures, Robeson did well in law school and made many friends at Columbia. He sat at the speakers' table as a guest of honor when the 1920 graduating class held its annual senior dinner. According to the class president, it was because "he was one of Columbia's most brilliant men."[2]

That same year, a young woman who would have a major impact on Paul Robeson entered his life. Photos show Eslanda Cardozo Goode, called Essie by friends and family, as an exotic and beautiful young woman with a heart-shaped face and pencil-thin eyebrows. She denied that she was pretty and described herself as "short and thick." She stood only as high as one of Robeson's broad shoulders. He was more than six feet tall with the strong neck and build of an athlete and a warm, outgoing smile.

When Essie met Robeson, other young women in Harlem were swarming all over him. "I thought since all the girls were making such a fuss over him, I would try being casual and indifferent," she said. "It was just one of those things—it worked."[3]

Like Robeson, Essie had gone to college on a scholarship. She had been born in Washington, D.C., but had moved to Harlem in 1905 after her father died. Essie's family valued education just as Robeson's did. Her father, a government clerk in the War Department, had gone to Northwestern University. Her grandfather was Francis Lewis Cardozo, the black secretary of state of South Carolina during the Reconstruction period after the Civil War. Cardozo had also founded the first school for blacks in South Carolina.

One day in August 1921, Paul and Essie decided to get married and rode a streetcar to Rye, New York, where they could marry without waiting for a license. But after the ceremony, they weren't ready to announce the news and make a home together, partly due to lack of money. Robeson was still a law student, and Essie had dropped out of medical school to work as an analytical chemist in a laboratory at Columbia Presbyterian Hospital.

But by Christmas, the situation had become embarrassing. As Essie told it: "When our friends saw that we seemed to be 'going together,' one or two went to Paul and told him he was making a mistake, that I was a fast New York woman. . . . Others came to me and told me that I was making a mistake, that football players never made anything of themselves later in life."[4]

Soon the two announced their marriage and had their own small apartment on 138th Street, and Essie began to push Robeson to take a step that would lead him into a new area, the world of theater. She persuaded him to take the lead role in *Simon the Cyrenian*, one of several plays written for blacks by the white poet Ridgely Torrence. The play was first produced in 1917, but in 1922 was being revived by the Harlem YMCA. In the play, Simon wants to lead a rebellion to rescue Jesus from the Romans but is stopped by Christ himself. Simon ends up carrying Jesus' cross for him.

Robeson admitted to "being literally dragged into rehearsal" by the play's director.[5] Even so, his performance won praise from the playwright and others, but Robeson went to school the next day, thinking more about briefs and judges than scripts and producers. The incident was a good example of the influence that Essie had on Robeson. Convinced of his talents, she spurred him on to new goals.

Although he had other managers over the years, she often directed his financial and business affairs.

After *Simon*, Robeson appeared in yet another play by a white playwright, Mary Hoyt Wiborg. But this drama, *Taboo*, was put on professionally at the Sam Harris Theater in New York. Robeson played a voodoo king opposite Margaret Wycherly, a well-known English actress who played his queen. The setting was a Southern plantation with some flashback scenes in Africa. One photo from the play shows Robeson, posing as a native in a garish sarong with a foot-tall wig of tangled, bushy hair. It was not an outstanding drama, but for Robeson it represented a decent way to make a living while struggling to make ends meet as a student.

During the summer of 1922, the play was renamed *Voodoo* and toured England, this time with Robeson playing opposite an English actress and director, Mrs. Patrick Campbell. She urged Robeson to think about playing the lead in *Othello*. But Robeson had his mind on the law. "At this time I was an aspiring lawyer, believing that to succeed would help raise my people, the black people of the world. Theater and concerts were furthest from my mind; this trip was just a lark. Instead of waiting on tables in hotels to earn money, I was being paid twenty pounds or so a week for expenses to walk on a stage, say a few lines, sing a song or two. Just too good for words."[6]

"A damn fine man with real brains"

When Robeson graduated from Columbia Law School in 1923, the Black Renaissance, an awakening of black culture and art, was in full bloom in Harlem. Thousands of blacks had moved North to find jobs. Although they were barred from many occupations, some found that the entertainment world and the arts offered an avenue of success. Black artists like Duke Ellington, Louis Armstrong, Bessie Smith, and Ethel Waters drew packed audiences to Harlem nightclubs like the Cotton Club, Connie's, and Small's Paradise. White intellectuals and the society crowd flocked to Harlem to hear the best of jazz and later swing and boogie-woogie.

Harlem was also home to many black thinkers and writers: the poet James Weldon Johnson, who wrote for the New York stage; Countee Cullen, who made his reputation with his first book of poems, *Color;* and W. E. B. Du Bois, who devoted his writing to pleading the cause of black people.

A number of white writers fascinated by the Harlem scene produced books or plays about blacks, like the ones that Paul Robeson had performed in. Robeson also sang at the Cotton Club and had a singing role with a quartet in a black musical, *Shuffle Along,* that took New York by storm in the early 1920s.

After graduation, Robeson had hesitated about opening a legal practice. For month after month he waited and watched while his white fellow graduates got jobs, and Essie Robeson continued to work at Columbia-Presbyterian Hospital. Robeson was offered a political job but declined to take it. Essie must have realized the difficulties involved in a black person's attempting a legal career during those years, but she was growing frustrated. "He was not the person to think out what he would do or wanted to do and then go out and try to do it. . . . He idled away month after month, waiting for something that would interest him to come along," Essie said about that trying time. [1]

Then a lawyer in downtown New York, someone who had been a trustee of Rutgers, invited Robeson to join his prominent law firm. Although Robeson was asked to write briefs on several cases, other lawyers in the office objected to having a black on the staff. As a way of sidestepping the growing storm, the partner who brought Robeson into the firm suggested that he might want to open a branch of the office in Harlem, but Robeson declined to take what would have been a difficult step.

A practice in Harlem based on divorce cases and other minor legal matters would have offered little challenge and few financial rewards to Robeson, who had had great ambition since childhood. It was easy to doubt whether a black man could ever succeed as a lawyer. The final blow came when a white secretary refused to take dictation from Robeson. So after a short time, Robeson left his first and only job in the field of law. Haunted by his desire for a career in which he would have a chance for success, he returned to waiting for the world to open up to him. Essie was upset when he told her: "I'll wait a little, something will turn up." [2] Later she decided he was simply being careful about what he would do with his life.

It wasn't long before Robeson began to look to the stage as the next step in his career. His performance in *Simon the*

Cyrenian had impressed some pioneering theater people who would change his life—the Provincetown Players. The players got their name from the wharfside theater where the group began in Provincetown, Massachusetts. Eventually, they turned a rundown brownstone house in Greenwich Village in New York City into a 150-seat theater.

Although the theater was off-Broadway and very small, the players sparked a revolution in theater. They included many writers and actors who would leave a mark on American arts: Edna St. Vincent Millay, Edmund Wilson, Edna Ferber, e. e. cummings, and Susan Glaspell. But the person who had the most impact on Robeson's life was the playwright, Eugene O'Neill.

Later considered America's greatest dramatist, O'Neill went on to write such artistic triumphs as *Mourning Becomes Electra, Desire Under the Elms, The Iceman Cometh*, and *Long Day's Journey Into Night* and won the Nobel Prize in literature. Already O'Neill had won the Pulitzer Prize.

Robeson was hired for $75 a week to play the lead in O'Neill's *All God's Chillun Got Wings*, one of the many plays that white authors were then writing about blacks. O'Neill considered Robeson to be "a young fellow with considerable experience, wonderful presence and voice, full of ambition and a damn fine man personally with real brains."[3]

Even before the play reached the stage, the public had read its plot in a national magazine. The drama focuses on Ella Downey, a white woman raised in New York in a racially mixed neighborhood. She has a child by her white boyfriend who then deserts her. To escape the life of a prostitute, she marries Jim Harris, a black friend from her childhood. But she can't cope with white racism and feels rejected by Harris's family. Meanwhile, Harris graduates from high school but fails in his goal of becoming a lawyer and keeps muffing key examinations. Finally Ella goes crazy.

The play has been criticized for molding Jim Harris into

(29)

a stereotype that many find objectionable. A weak but good-hearted man, Harris doesn't know how to fight back. But still, in *Chillun*, O'Neill was trying to deal with racial discrimination. As O'Neill told one interviewer: "Ella of the play loved her husband, but could not love him as a woman would a man, though she wanted to, because of her background and her inherited racial prejudice. ... . Prejudices racial, social, religious—life is hard and bitter enough without, in addition, burdening ourselves with prejudices."[4]

The New York newspapers, sensing that they could turn O'Neill's play into something that would sell more papers, wrote story after story playing on racial prejudice and focusing on a final scene in the play when Ella collapses beside Jim's chair and kisses his hand. When it was learned that a white woman, Mary Blair, would indeed play Ella, a news service sent out a photograph of her with the headline: White Actress Kisses Negro's Hand.

The *New York Morning Telegraph* and the *American* ran wild stories with no attribution except for words such as "rumor has it" or "it is said." Some articles claimed that wealthy patrons planned to cut off funds for the Provincetown Players. Others claimed that Blair, worried about hurting her career, had quit the play. In fact, neither was true. Blair held fast, and two rich patrons actually increased their gifts to the playhouse.

The city of New York refused to step into the dispute because the theater was an unlicensed club with admission limited to its subscribers. So the *American* wrote a story saying that the mayor could shut the play down if it could be shown that it might incite race riots.

As soon as the theater group denied one story, another was written. An official of the theater pleaded in one article: "We are producing the play because it is beautiful. ... Some people may storm our doors, but if they wait and see the play, they will go away humble."[5]

Still, many well-known blacks in New York City objected to the play. The Rev. A. Clayton Powell, pastor of the Abyssinian Baptist Church and father of a congressman, said it was "harmful because it intimates that we are desirous of marrying white women."[6]

But one famous black defended the play—W. E. B. Du Bois, later a close friend of Paul Robeson. Du Bois noted that blacks were sensitive about how they were portrayed in literature because for years: "Any mention of Negro blood or Negro life in America for a century has been occasion for an ugly picture, a dirty allusion, a nasty comment or a pessimistic forecast."

Du Bois went on: "Happy is the artist that breaks through any of these shells, for his is the kingdom of eternal beauty. . . . Eugene O'Neill is bursting through."[7]

Robeson, Mary Blair, and the play's director, James Light, all received vicious letters, including some from the Ku Klux Klan. "A great many were obscene or threatening or both, but Mary and Paul didn't see the largest part because we began holding them back," Light said.[8]

During the furor, O'Neill stood by his leading man, Paul Robeson: "I believe he can portray the character better than any other actor could. That's all there is to it."[9] O'Neill pointed out that Robeson had already appeared in New York and London in *Voodoo* with a white actress. There were no race riots then, O'Neill noted, and no newspaper riots either.

How did all this affect Robeson? Already he had endured prejudice in school, on the football field, and in the world of law. At such a young age to be the center of national protests must have shaped his thinking about racial discrimination and the difficulties that blacks had in pursuing careers in any field.

"Objections to *All God's Chillun* are rather well known," Robeson said later. "Most of them have been so foolish that to attempt to answer them is to waste time. The best answer is that audiences that came to scoff went away in tears, moved by a sincere and terrifically tragic drama."[10]

During rehearsals Robeson leaned heavily on O'Neill and Light to improve his acting and to help him overcome his stage fright. When Robeson had trouble with a passage in the play, Light went over it word by word until Robeson worked it out. Gradually, Robeson formed a concept of what Jim Harris stood for.

Then there was a new development. The playhouse had to delay *All God's Chillun* because Mary Blair got sick. The play, planned to open in March, was delayed until May, and in its place the theater staged a revival of O'Neill's *The Emperor Jones,* this time with Robeson in the title role. This turned out to be good luck for the players. Suddenly, the controversy over *All God's Chillun* died down, and Robeson could prove himself in a play that was a known success.

On the one hand, *The Emperor Jones* was tainted by stereotypes, portraying blacks as superstitious and half-civilized. But the main character, Brutus Jones, is also intelligent and dignified. Robeson's height of six feet two inches and his 200-pound build were well suited to the part of Jones, a Pullman porter from the United States who becomes the dictator of a group of natives on a tropical island. As the play opens, the natives are rising against Jones and he has fled into the jungle.

Although reviewers came prepared to be highly critical, the production was a triumph. They found Robeson had a voice that was "unmatched in the American theater."[11]

After the opening at a party held over the theater, O'Neill played for hours on a drum from *Emperor.* The playwright, Robeson, and other partygoers took off their shirts to compare their muscles. The raucous celebration continued until neighbors sent a policeman to complain about the noise.

At last, *All God's Chillun* was ready for the stage. But a final obstacle arose late in the afternoon of May 15 just before the play's opening. The chief clerk for the mayor phoned to tell the players that the city had rejected their application to use child actors in a scene in which black and white youngsters play games together. No amount of arguing could change minds down at city hall.

As Robeson and the other actors stepped out on stage, they were anxious. But gradually they fell into the mood of the play. According to O'Neill, the lack of any rioting or strife was almost a disappointment. When the fateful scene occurred and Blair's lips touched Robeson's wrist, the audience was somber and quiet.

Reviewers felt the same kind of letdown with the play itself. Heywood Broun called it "a very tiresome play."[12] Alexander Woollcott said the play was "a strained, wanton and largely unbelievable tragedy . . . it did not come to life truly and vividly on the stage."[13] But Paul Robeson himself, his movement on stage, his voice, his mood, impressed most critics despite what they thought of the play. George Jean Nathan said he was "one of the most thoroughly eloquent, impressive and convincing actors that I have looked at and listened to in almost twenty years of professional theatre-going."[14]

Despite the mixed reviews, *All God's Chillun* was performed one hundred times and made money. All the wild publicity about the play only served to draw bigger crowds. Among those who watched Robeson perform for O'Neill was a slightly overweight, bespectacled drama critic for the *New York Herald*—Alexander Woollcott, known for his sharp wit. He led a circle of friends called the Algonquin Round Table, after the New York hotel where the group met for lunch.

Robeson's success on stage won him friends in Woollcott's crowd, which included other entertainers and columnists, people like Heywood Broun and Robert Benchley, valuable friends for a young actor. Robeson became a popular player at the group's all-night poker parties and attended parties at Woollcott's home. Other black artists and writers, such as James Weldon Johnson, Walter White, and Florence Mills, were also Algonquin favorites.

At one party, Heywood Broun suggested that Robeson give a public concert of the black spirituals he sang for his friends. Robeson had sung in some performances of *Emperor Jones*, but he was reluctant to do a concert because he'd never had voice lessons. He also didn't think that anyone would pay to hear music that could be heard for free on Sunday in any Harlem church. But Broun urged him to hire the hall and promised to provide the audience.

Robeson held back even though he needed the money. By then *Emperor* and *Chillun* had closed. For a while, his only job was the lead in *Body and Soul*, a low-budget B-movie in which he played a Georgia minister.

But a chance encounter gave Robeson the inspiration he needed. One day in March 1925, at 135th Street and Seventh Avenue, he bumped into Lawrence Brown, an American pianist whom Robeson had met in Europe. When not working as an accompanist, Brown spent his time scoring black spirituals. Robeson invited Brown to a party at the apartment of James Light. Brown played piano while Robeson sang Brown's arrangements of "Swing Low, Sweet Chariot" and "Every Time I Feel the Spirit." Brown even joined in with his tenor voice.

That night the group, including Essie, persuaded Robeson to give his first concert, one devoted to black spirituals. A $100 deposit was put down on the Greenwich Village Theater for Sunday night, April 19. Broun drummed up interest in his newspaper column. Novelist Carl Van Vechten nailed up posters and passed out handbills, and writer Walter White promoted the concert through the Associated Negro Press. Thanks to all this publicity, the theater was sold out to a well-dressed uptown crowd, and scalpers offered tickets at $25 a seat.

Somewhat nervously, Robeson and Brown walked on stage and led off with "Go Down Moses." After that came "Swing Low, Sweet Chariot," "Joshua Fit the Battle of Jericho," and other spirituals. Robeson also sang the work song "Water Boy" that later became one of his classics. Loud applause soon relieved his anxiety, and at the end, there was wild clapping until they did encores. Finally, the house lights had to be turned on so that everyone would go home.

The critics were impressed, including those who weren't from Broun's paper. "Mr. Robeson is a singer of genuine power. . . . His Negro spirituals hold in them a cry from the depths, a universal humanism that touches the heart," wrote the *New York Times*.[15]

Suddenly Robeson was in demand as a singer, and that summer he and Lawrence Brown were signed for a tour beginning in 1926. Meanwhile, Paul and Essie Robeson were bound for London where he would perform in a British version of *The Emperor Jones*.

"In the most aristocratic circles"

In September 1925, Robeson and Essie arrived in London for the opening of *The Emperor Jones*. Quickly, the Robesons found a new freedom from the racial bias that barred them from certain restaurants, hotels, and neighborhoods in America. The British were much less likely to treat them differently because they were black. After a night as *Emperor Jones*, Robeson could drop across the street from the theater to the Ivy restaurant for a meal. In fact, he and his friends, black or white, could eat at any restaurant in the city without fear of rejection or discrimination. While living in New York City, he had been almost completely limited to restaurants in Harlem or Greenwich Village.

On the weekends, the Robesons spent pleasant days at seaside resorts and booked first-class seats on trains. It was startling after the many times in the United States when the lighter-skinned Essie had to buy their train tickets in order to book decent seats.

Of course, serious racial discrimination was strong in parts of the British Empire, particularly in the colonies in Africa and India where the white British ruled and natives of those countries served. The Robesons knew about this, and Essie Robeson found the British "self-righteous" at times. As she said: "They were doing even worse to their own colonial peoples in their colonies, mind you, but they were nice in England."[1]

London's society opened its drawing rooms, banquet halls, and yachts to the Robesons. "I found myself moving a great deal in the most aristocratic circles," Robeson said. It was a friendly and yet an intellectual atmosphere. "And, to an American Negro, the marked respect for law and order which is common among all classes throughout the British Isles was especially pleasing," Robeson found.[2]

Through the Provincetown Players, the Robesons met Emma Goldman, a Russian-born anarchist who sometimes lectured on drama. Goldman, nicknamed "Red Emma" by her enemies, had been deported from the United States in 1919 for organizing strikes and anti-war rallies. Along with 247 other "Reds," she was shipped off to Russia, which gave the group a warm welcome. She expected to find in the Soviet state the revolution she had always dreamed about. But she soon grew upset with the growth in bureaucracy, lack of free speech, and political persecution in that country. She eventually ended up in London.

Goldman cooked dinner for the Robesons and other friends, and in return Robeson sang to entertain everyone. "Essie was a delightful person, and Paul fascinated everyone," Goldman said. "Nothing I had been told about his singing adequately expressed the moving quality of his voice. Paul was also a lovable personality, entirely free from the self-importance of the star and as natural as a child."[3]

Soon, the Robesons had a large list of friends, blacks and whites, including artists, writers, and actors. The only troubling note was that *The Emperor Jones* closed almost as soon as it opened in October. The public found the beating of the tom-toms during the play nervewracking and sometimes laughed in the wrong places. British reviewers were critical, even though they gave Robeson good notices. "I couldn't understand what they were talking about," said

Robeson. "I knew nothing about the technique of acting, or about the actor's art. I knew when I saw good acting, but I didn't know how it was achieved."4

When the play closed, Robeson and his wife stayed on in Europe where they felt freedom from racial prejudice. After another month the English winter set in, and they moved on to the milder French Riviera, then packed with famous American and European writers and actors: F. Scott Fitzgerald, Robert Benchley, Ernest Hemingway, and many others.

With a friend's help, the Robesons found a low-cost hotel in Villefranche-sur-Mer, a small French town between Nice and Monte Carlo, on the Mediterranean Riviera. In the tiny village at the foot of the Alps, they had spectacular views of the sea and spent their days skiing in nearby mountains or climbing crooked little streets among shops and brightly painted villas.

On the Riviera, just as in London, they met new friends and visited with old ones. One day in Nice, Robeson met Claude McKay, a black poet who was working on one of the first best-sellers ever produced by a black writer, *Home to Harlem*, the story of a black soldier returning home after World War I. McKay, in turn, introduced them to Max Eastman, an American writer who founded some socialist and anti-war magazines. For many evenings in hotel rooms or in the cafés and restaurants of Nice, McKay, Robeson, and Eastman talked about Russia and socialism, as well as news that Robeson brought from Harlem. Robeson also sang for the little group in what Eastman called his "solemnly celestial voice."

Just like Goldman, Eastman had recently returned from Russia. He had married the daughter of a Soviet official. Eastman had written a book critical of Russia's dictator Joseph Stalin. According to Eastman, the last wish of Lenin, the leader of the Russian Revolution, had been that Stalin be removed from office. Because of the book, Eastman was condemned by the Russian leaders and by left-wing sympathizers in the United States. But what Robeson heard about Russia excited his interest in that country. Soon he began studying Russian himself.

Later Eastman wrote a biography in which he discussed Robeson and Essie, whom Eastman called Robeson's "strong-minded wife." "I've always thought she was at the wheel when Paul, a man with a gentle heart and magnanimous understanding of America's slow progress toward race equality, veered from his path, and became a blustering yet manipulated advocate of totalitarian tyranny over all the races," Eastman said.[5]

Of course, Eastman had become a conservative who clashed with people like the Robesons who sympathized with Russia. But Eastman wasn't the only person to note Essie's role in Robeson's life. Many commented on her determination, energy, and spirit, and some wondered what influence she had on Robeson's political thinking.

"Some found her pushy, others hard, and still others, charming," said Essie's granddaughter, Susan Robeson, in a biography of her grandfather. "But above it all, she was brilliant and found herself at odds with society's definition of the proper place for a woman—much less a black woman who was a scientist, anthropologist, journalist and world traveler."[6]

With regret, the Robesons finally left Europe for the United States. But a new chapter was about to open in Paul Robeson's life. The voice that charmed his new friends on the Riviera would thrill crowds in concert halls across the United States.

Robeson had sung for years, in church, at schools, and in friends' homes. But he had never had formal voice training. Yet in the winter of 1926, he opened a nationwide concert tour with his pianist and composer Lawrence Brown.

From the beginning, Essie took charge, handling let-

(39)

ters, buying rail tickets, arranging interviews with reporters, and paying hotel bills. She was frail and her health was not always strong, but she was hardworking and ambitious. Just how determined she could be was revealed on one tour when she took several thousand dollars out of a bank in New York and walked down Fifth Avenue to shop. As she left a store, a strange white man pushed her against a window and demanded her money. It flashed through her mind that the money wasn't hers, it belonged to Robeson and Brown.

Next she heard the loud voice of a woman yelling furiously, "How dare you! I won't give it to you!" "The woman was me—it was my voice!" Essie said. "I had seized the man, thrown him down, and was jumping on him, yelling furiously to an astonished and sympathetic crowd."[7]

Many triumphs marked the early days of the first tour, including once in Chicago when Robeson arrived in late February to find that almost no advertising had been done for his concert at Orchestra Hall. On stage before a half-filled auditorium, Robeson determined that he would do his best anyway. Encore after encore followed, and the next morning a critic for the *Chicago Herald-Examiner* wrote: "I have just heard the finest of all Negro voices and one of the most beautiful in the world, and those fortunate ones who were present last night in Orchestra Hall, when Paul Robeson made his first Chicago appearance, will testify that I do not exaggerate."[8]

Robeson began to study the spirituals he was singing. He believed that black slaves had based most of their music on the Old Testament because of the liberation theme of the stories of Moses, Daniel, Joseph, and Joshua. America's slaves saw hope in the stories of how God delivered the Israelites.

But Robeson found that blacks in the 1920s did not all enjoy this music. "I found a special eagerness among the younger and, I am sorry to say, the more intelligent Negroes, to dismiss the spiritual as something beneath their new pride in their race. It is as if they wanted to put it behind them as something to be ashamed of—something that tied them to a past in which their forefathers were slaves," he said.[9]

But Robeson believed that the songs that thrilled him as a child were a form of poetry that belonged in the concert hall. "By accepting the white man's music," Robeson warned, "we are passing out of the scene as creators and interpreters of the finest expression and loftiest we have to offer."[10]

During their tours, the Robesons fought many battles with discrimination in hotels and restaurants. In one western city, their local concert manager told them they could not go to a modern first-class hotel where they had reservations but had to stay in the home of a nice black family.

When Essie demanded to know why, the manager admitted that the hotel would not take them because they were black. Essie told him no hotel, no concert, and when the manager threatened to sue them, she threatened to sue the hotel. "Paul and Larry were amused at my annoyance, and just sat quietly and watched me hold forth," Essie said. "When the manager appealed directly to them, they said innocently, 'She's our representative and has charge of us. Sorry!'"

The hotel gave them the suite they had reserved but asked them to use the freight elevator and to eat in their rooms for fear that other guests would leave if they saw blacks in the hotel. Later in a passenger elevator, they were mobbed by guests seeking autographs. "I shall always remember," Essie said, "a man and wife and their three children, a charming family, who said to Paul, 'Mr. Robeson we came to the hotel for dinner, hoping to catch a glimpse of you in the dining room. It's very exclusive and selfish of you to eat in your rooms.'"[11]

Another time, they arrived in Boston one winter morning after an overnight train ride to find Robeson had caught cold. A taxi took them to a low-cost hotel which refused to rent a room to blacks. For a while they wandered aimlessly in their taxi. Finally, they went to the best hotel in town, which took them in. Robeson went straight to bed.

When he woke up a few hours later, he sounded worse than ever. He told Brown that he had to call off the Symphony Hall concert. But Essie and Brown urged him to try. "Paul was so frightened that he walked on the stage in a trance," Essie said. "He never sang so badly in his life. His rich, lovely voice was tight and hard and unrecognizable."[12]

Brown was crushed because Boston was his home and he had hoped to be a smashing success there. Robeson threatened never to sing there again. Surprisingly, the audience was kind, and the newspaper critics noted that Robeson had a cold.

But the experience led Essie to conclude that Robeson needed some training. She believed that professionally trained singers could do well even when they were sick. She contacted Theresa Armitage, a voice teacher who had taught Essie when she was in high school. According to Essie, Robeson didn't even know the range of his voice— how high he could sing and how low he could sing—until Armitage showed him. "You just think your range is short," Armitage told him. "It's all of two and a quarter octaves, which is long enough for any reasonable person."[13]

It was during these concerts that Essie told Robeson she wanted to have a baby. According to a biography of Robeson that Essie later wrote, he was reluctant to agree because of her health problems, but she insisted. On November 2, 1927, after a very difficult birth, their baby son was born. He looked a great deal like his father. "Even his baby voice was deep," Essie said. "No one ever asked his name; everyone simply and naturally called him Paul."[14]

"Ol' Man River, he just keeps rolling along"

In 1926, the famous Broadway composer Jerome Kern created a musical based on the novel *Show Boat* by Edna Ferber and wrote "Ol' Man River," a song designed just for Paul Robeson.

The play spans twenty years on a Mississippi showboat, the *Cotton Blossom,* run by Captain Andy Hawks. Some twenty songs were written for the musical, but the best was "Ol' Man River," sung by a black laborer, Joe, the role picked out for Robeson.

After finishing the song, Kern dashed to the Robeson apartment in Harlem to have Robeson sing it. The Robesons were excited about the play, but plans for the production were delayed several times. When *Show Boat* finally came to Broadway in December 1927, Robeson was on a concert tour that prevented his appearing in the show.

It was unfortunate, because during these years of concert touring, Robeson had struggled to find the right play, suited to his talents. He had one brief run in New York in a play called *Black Boy,* about a prizefighter. The play received some good reviews but failed to draw an audience.

He also appeared briefly in *Porgy,* a play by DuBose and Dorothy Heyward, that tells the story of Porgy, a crippled beggar who becomes involved in a murder. Robeson played the villain Crown and sang several musical numbers. But Robeson quit the show after four weeks because singing jazz strained his voice.

Like many black actors then, Robeson often had to ignore what a play was about or how it portrayed blacks. "What mattered was the opportunity, which came so seldom to our folks, of having a part—any part—to play on the stage or in the movies; and for a Negro actor to be offered a starring role—well, that was a rare stroke of fortune indeed!" he said. [1]

Later on, he refused to view an acting job solely in terms of what it paid. He rejected those roles based on black stereotypes. In some ways, Joe in *Show Boat* was one of those same old hackneyed black characters. But in the spring of 1928 when Robeson was offered the role in the London production of *Show Boat*, the Robesons were thrilled. Work in London meant a chance to return to the England they had grown to love and an opportunity for Robeson to advance his career. Their baby, now nicknamed Pauli, was left with his grandmother, and the Robesons sailed for England.

Show Boat was destined to be one of the most spectacular productions ever at the Theater Royal in London's Drury Lane. A cast of 160 actors was assembled and decked out in 1,000 costumes purchased at the then extravagant sum of $30,000. However, from the first rehearsals, this production was marked by tremendous upheaval, according to Cedric Hardwicke, the British actor who played Captain Andy of the *Cotton Blossom*. Crew after crew of actors and actresses tried out for parts for a few days and then were fired by the dissatisfied producers.

Many British actors signed for the play were confused by its American slang, and Hardwicke, who had never danced or sung on stage before, had to do a polka, sing a chorus, and play the violin. A troupe of black actresses, playing residents of Mississippi riverfront towns, was brought at great cost from New York to make the play more authentic. The producer was furious when they showed up at dress rehearsal for some strange reason wearing dead-white makeup.

But when Robeson showed up to play Joe, the situation calmed down. After a few more rehearsals, the play opened in April 1928. The early scenes were tuneful and pleasant but not very memorable. Then Robeson as Joe the Riverman began toting bales of cotton across the wharfside scenery. Robeson was only thirty, but his hair had been grayed and his back was bent as if he carried the pain of all black slaves that had once lived along the Mississippi.

His mighty voice rolled out across the audience, carrying them back to the Old South. That evening he became Ol' Man River. It was a song that probably more than any other would belong to Paul Robeson. Although the audience didn't know it then, the song would become his lifelong political statement, and over and over throughout the years, he would change its words to suit the message he brought to the world about racism and injustice.

The audience, some of whom waited in line twenty-four hours to buy tickets, sat stunned for a moment and then clapped wildly. In just a few moments of music, *Show Boat* had become a smash hit. Critics were crazy about the show, and in particular about Robeson. As one London writer put it: "The thing that will be remembered first and last—the thing that held it all together and will be on everybody's lips before many days are over, is the song of 'Old Man River.' It is there in every form, given out gravely in the rich bass of Mr. Paul Robeson."[2]

As Cedric Hardwicke put it: "The first-night notices told that Robeson had captured London."[3] The other actors were relieved. Their jobs were saved. All the fears that London might not understand a distinctly American play were gone. The play settled into a long and prosperous run.

Amid all this success, one dispute almost spoiled everything. Before coming to London, Robeson had signed a contract to perform in a black musical revue in New York. But after receiving an advance payment on his contract, he'd heard nothing more about the revue.

Then suddenly during his smash run in *Show Boat*, the producer of the revue demanded that he return to New York to go on stage there. Robeson refused. It wasn't the question of money, he said, he thought he could make more money in New York. But the type of music he would have to sing in the revue would be much like that in *Porgy*, the jazz and blues that strained his voice. He'd signed the contract at a weak moment, a time when he needed the money and when Essie had been sick, he said. And of course, his exciting success in London played a role in his refusal to return to New York.

He returned the advance money and Essie even went back to New York to work out a settlement, but the revue producer went to court. The dispute took some time to iron out. None of this seemed to keep the public from identifying Robeson with *Show Boat*, and after his London success, he was offered the role of Joe again some years later in a New York revival of the play.

Edna Ferber, who wrote the novel *Show Boat*, had objected strongly when the revival of the play was proposed in New York in 1932. No one, she said, would go to see it again, and she even refused to attend the opening. As the rest of her family left for the theater, she told them, "I am not one to enjoy seeing something I love killed before my eyes."[4]

But that night she went out for a walk and was drawn to the theater. She saw crowds milling around outside and was told at the box office that even standing room tickets were sold out. Ferber peeked through the theater door just as

Robeson came on stage to sing "Ol' Man River." Members of the audience stood and howled, shouted and stamped their feet. "The show stopped. They called him back again and again. Other actors came out and made motions and their lips moved, but the bravos of the audience drowned all other sounds," she said.5

"Go back, what in heaven's name for?"

After the London run of *Show Boat*, the Robesons stayed in England, deciding to make it their home. Essie rented a suburban house overlooking Hampstead Heath, an open area of grassy hills and trees where Londoners loved to walk, ride horses and fly kites. Eventually, Essie's mother and baby Pauli came to England to live with them.

Meanwhile, the Robesons became the darlings of London's upper crust. Nearly every day, new invitations arrived to parties and lunches with aristocrats, government officials, or celebrities like author H. G. Wells and playwright George Bernard Shaw. Robeson began to think about politics and world affairs and formed new opinions about racism and social change. Just before *Show Boat* closed, he went to lunch at Britain's House of Commons with members of Parliament from the left-wing Labour party. The former prime minister of England, Ramsay MacDonald, and Robeson discussed the British colonies in India and Africa. Robeson shared the view of Labour party members that Britain should leave these countries.

Later, Robeson went to a party in England, where the wife of U.S. President Calvin Coolidge was a guest. The event, Robeson said, helped shape his views of socialism, the political movement that advocates government control of production and sale of goods. Mrs. Coolidge sat next to playwright George Bernard Shaw, a member of the socialist Fabian Society. "She talked loudly, aggressively, and she was crude in her reactions to Shaw when he expounded on socialism," Robeson said. [1]

But Robeson didn't know what to say when Shaw asked him for his own opinions. Although he had talked with friends who had visited Russia and observed its Marxist-socialist government, Robeson had not thought much about socialism before. But a seed was planted in his mind.

Later, when Robeson looked back on this time in England, he praised the British. He decided to live in England, he said, for the same reasons that many millions of blacks left the Deep South for other parts of the country. "In those happy days, had someone suggested that my home should be 'back home' in Jim Crow America I would have thought he was out of his mind. Go back—well what in heaven's name for?" [2]

Even thousands of miles away from home, the racism of America touched him. The Robesons were particularly hurt about an annual Fourth of July party that the U.S. ambassador held for Americans in England, except for blacks. In their twelve years in England, the Robesons were never invited to this celebration of the birth of their native land. "We were invited to many of the most interesting and historic homes in England, and the English people felt that Paul was a distinguished American artist and person, yet our own Embassy never included us officially or socially," Essie Robeson said. [3]

In the spring of 1929, Robeson, Essie, and Lawrence Brown went on a concert tour of Central Europe. Robeson was wildly popular in Vienna and also in Prague, Czechoslovakia, and Budapest, Hungary. In Prague, the touring trio were treated with deep respect by the American minister to Czechoslovakia, a Mr. Einstein, who attended the concert and invited the Robesons to supper. After the concert, the Robesons and Brown were driven to the American Legation in a limousine with a U.S. flag on the hood. "Larry, Paul and I agreed then that this was one time we could feel proud of our flag," said Essie. "Mr. Einstein never knew what he did for us. We had a rather low opinion of Americans abroad just then."[4]

The trip also led Robeson to a new interest in foreign languages, and he soon began to study German. Throughout his life he became fluent in some twenty foreign languages, including several from Africa, Chinese, Russian, and Arabic. He could learn a language in a week, according to his son, Pauli.

As Robeson listened to Slavic and Hungarian folk songs on this trip, he found them similar to Negro spirituals and African music. He began to study the folk music of other countries and added some of these songs to his concerts. Later he found that many folk songs are based on a pentatonic or five-toned scale, a scale that uses only the black notes of the piano.

While Robeson had been in *Show Boat,* the actor Maurice Browne saw him perform and suggested that they do a play together in London, hopefully Shakespeare's drama, *Othello.* For many years, Robeson had dreamed as well of playing Othello, the Moorish general in the service of Venice, who is enticed to believe that his bride Desdemona has been unfaithful. He strangles her and then kills himself after he learns his suspicions are unfounded.

After returning to London following his concert tour and also singing at Carnegie Hall in New York, Robeson set to work on *Othello.* He bought copies of all Shakespeare's plays plus books on the playwright and began to study. He practiced with Old English texts so that he could give words like "chance" and "demand" the proper British accent. Some seven months before the play opened, he had learned all his lines.

As rehearsals began, a racist controversy, similar to the one about *All God's Chillun,* started in the British press. Letters from women newspaper readers complained about a black man playing opposite the white actress Peggy Ashcroft as Desdemona. The controversy was not nearly as heated as the earlier one in New York, but still Robeson was upset. "In my heart I thought that in London trouble could not possibly arise on racial grounds," Robeson said.[5]

Nervously, Robeson backed away from Ashcroft in their rehearsals, although she told the press that the racial question was silly: "I see no difference in being kissed by Paul Robeson and being kissed by any other man."[6]

But there was another side to the debate about Robeson's *Othello*—one that has continued to the present day. Did Shakespeare mean for Othello to be portrayed by a black man or by a dark-skinned Arab? The actual title of the play is *The Tragedie of Othello, Moor of Venice,* and the argument focused on whether "Moor" refers to an Arab or what those in Shakespeare's time called a "blackamoor." Robeson told the press that he saw Othello's color as a vital issue in the play. He believed that the play was a tragedy brought on in part by racial conflict.

In Shakespeare's time, he said, there was probably no big distinction between Moors and brown or black. "In Shakespeare's own time and throughout the Restoration, . . . the part was played as a black man," Robeson said.

It wasn't until the nineteenth century that Othello was thought of as brown-skinned, Robeson said. "I feel that had to do with the fact that at that time Africa was the slave center of the world, and people wanted to forget the ancient glory of the Ethiopians."[7]

Browne, who played the evil Iago who tells Othello lies about Desdemona, said that in rehearsals Robeson spoke Shakespeare's verse almost as well as he sang spirituals. "In the jealousy scenes he—literally—foamed at the mouth; I used to wonder whether one day he might not seize Iago

(51)

and pluck out my arm."[8] Unfortunately, during rehearsals portions of the play were cut, and some words were changed to more modern English. The intent was to make the play easier to understand, but Robeson was upset at the cuts and found them difficult to work with.

On May 29, 1930, an audience packed with celebrities crowded the Savoy Theatre in London. The curtains swept back to reveal a highly unusual set for a Shakespearean drama. Darkness shrouded the stage, and most of the action took place at the top of two sets of stairs. The modern scenery gave the play a remote, frigid tone. The cast wore the brocades and velvets traditional with Shakespeare. Robeson had a beard and mustache. His massive costume and wide puffed sleeves trimmed in fur made him look huge and bulky in sharp contrast with the delicate Peggy Ashcroft.

Some felt that Robeson as Othello drew back and shrank away from Ashcroft. Some felt he moved across the stage like a panther, but others said he dragged himself around. But whatever the flaws, after the last words were spoken, the audience shouted its approval and demanded twenty curtain calls. Spectators cried out for Robeson to speak. He said simply: "I took the part of Othello with much fear. Now I am so happy."[9]

Eight out of twelve London drama critics called Robeson magnificent. The London *Morning Post,* for example, said "there has been no Othello on our stage, certainly in forty years, to compare with his in dignity, simplicity and true passion."[10]

But some found him lacking. "He was the underdog from the start," said one critic. "The cares of 'Ol' Man River' were still upon him. He was a member of a subject race, still dragging the chains of his ancestors. He was not noble enough. He was not stark enough. He seemed to me to be a very depressed Othello."[11]

Among those who saw Robeson perform in London was Margaret Webster, actress and director who "thought him very bad."[12] Later Robeson told her that he had been so overwhelmed about doing Shakespeare and especially about playing in London with his American accent, that he had not done as well as he had hoped. But neither Webster nor Robeson were deterred by these failings. One day they would stage one of the most famous *Othello* productions of all time.

One drama critic whom Robeson met while he played Othello was Marie Seton, a woman who became a close friend and who later wrote a biography of him.

The fact that a black American had impressed London with his Othello and had played opposite a white woman besides was causing talk thousands of miles away. It was suggested that Robeson bring the play to New York. It would be more than a dozen years before that came to be.

"A little tin angel with no faults at all"

Suddenly Paul Robeson was an international star, sought after for concerts, movies, and plays on both sides of the Atlantic. While his career soared, however, the fortunes of many Americans fell. The stock market crashed, and the Depression gripped the United States. Although these financial problems spread worldwide, the Robesons in Europe were less affected.

But if money wasn't a problem for the Robesons, they had other troubles. By 1930, their marriage seemed to be falling apart. Hints of their problems emerged in a biography, *Paul Robeson, Negro,* that Essie wrote about Robeson shortly after they moved to England. The book itself created conflicts because Robeson didn't want Essie to write it. But the strong-willed Essie, who later wrote several other books, went ahead anyway and eventually the biography was published in 1930. In some ways, the book flatters Robeson, but in other ways it does not.

"The whole trouble," Robeson says to a friend in the biography, "is that Essie thinks she knows me, and she really doesn't know me at all. She thinks I'm a little tin angel with no faults at all, and so, of course, the book is stupid, uninteresting, and untrue."[1]

Paul contended that Essie thought he was brave, honest, and moral when he was none of those things. But although the biography glorified and praised many of Robeson's accomplishments, Essie also indicated she had pushed her husband into some of his successes, including his role in *Othello*. Essie also indicated that Robeson paid very little attention to his toddler son.

The Robesons' son, Paul, Jr., felt his mother's book was biased in part by her own practical, take-charge personality. "She was pragmatic, the kind of person who liked to get things done. He was a thinker; his mind was extraordinary. When you talked about going from A to Z, he would discuss all the many paths to getting there. She simply wanted to get from A to Z."[2]

Probably the most explosive problem in the Robeson marriage was the continuing rumors and stories about his involvement with other women. In the biography, Essie admitted suspecting that Robeson had been fascinated by other women and might have pursued his interest in some way. In 1930, they separated. Robeson took a London flat, and Essie, her mother, and Pauli traveled while Essie pursued her writing career.

Now on his own, Robeson made concert tours in the United States and England during 1931. He added classical music to his programs including works by Mozart, Beethoven, and others and some songs in Russian. The effort did not always succeed; one critic complained that he sang foreign music the same way that he sang spirituals. But already it was noted how fluent he was in Russian. The complex language gave him few problems.

Eventually, Robeson announced that he would not sing again in French, German, or Italian because he didn't understand the psychology or philosophy of the people who spoke those languages. "Their history has nothing in common with the history of my slave ancestors," he said. "But I know the wail of the Hebrew, and I feel the plaint of the

Russian. I understand both, as I do the philosophy of the Chinese, and I feel that both have much in common with the traditions of my own race."[3]

He appeared in Berlin in 1930 in an English-language production of *The Emperor Jones.* Although many in the audience did not understand his words, his acting vividly conveyed the plot of the story. A year later, he acted in another Eugene O'Neill drama, *The Hairy Ape,* in London. Reviews were good, but after only five performances, Robeson dropped out because of laryngitis, and the play was canceled.

In 1932, he appeared in the triumphant revival of *Show Boat* in New York. All the while, rumors flew through the press about Robeson's involvement with women friends. In May 1932, for example, one of London's Sunday tabloids, *The People,* printed a gossip column indicating that a famous society matron had been romantically involved with a black man and that the woman had been forced to leave England for a couple of years until the affair blew over. The column used no names, but to London high society it clearly referred to Paul Robeson and Lady Louis Mountbatten, closely tied to Britain's royal family.

The Mountbattens sued for libel and Lady Mountbatten denied in court that she had ever even met the man mentioned in the article. The mystery man was never identified in court as Paul Robeson. The Mountbattens won their suit, and *The People* had to apologize.

By the end of May, though, Essie Robeson had filed for divorce in New York courts. "It is all perfectly friendly, and we will keep on being friends, but we've seen so much of each other and both are just a bit tired and want our freedom," Essie told *The New York Times.*[4] Other newspapers hinted that Paul Robeson was planning to marry someone else.

But suddenly, Robeson's other romantic interest ended. By year's end, he and Essie had reconciled. "In balance," said Paul, Jr., "I think they stayed together because they needed one another. Together they were more than the sum of their separate parts. It was a difficult marriage because they were both very bright and very able and very different in the way that they thought. But they made a team."[5]

Meanwhile, Paul Robeson's career was entering a new stage, brought on from Hollywood's switch from the silent movie to talking pictures. By 1930, audiences were clamoring for films in which they could hear as well as see the characters. Producers hunted for fresh talent with good voices, and a natural place to find them was on Broadway. The trend also meant new jobs in movies for the black dancers, singers, and musicians who had become so popular in New York theaters and dance clubs. With his resonant, powerful voice, Robeson seemed like a natural star for the new sound films.

Early films with sound tracks featuring black stars had layered together musical numbers and spirituals with scenes of prayer meetings and cotton picking. "Hollywood can only visualize the plantation type of Negro," Robeson told a film magazine, "the Negro of 'Poor Old Joe' and 'Swanee Ribber.' It is as absurd to use that type to express the modern Negro as it would be to express modern England in the terms of an Elizabethan ballad."[6] Over the next few years, he tried to change these stereotypes, sometimes succeeding but also sometimes falling short of his goal.

His first movies drew only small audiences. There had been the silent film, *Body and Soul*, made in 1924, but in 1930 he made *Borderline* in Switzerland with a pioneer filmmaker. The movie, set in a border town between two countries, centered on two couples, one white and one black, and their racial and personal conflicts. Essie played Robeson's wife in the film.

Then in 1933, Robeson was signed for *The Emperor Jones*, a sound film based on the play that was one of his early successes in New York. For the first time, a black man starred in a film in which whites were supporting players. The film also demanded that the main character, a black man, show a wide range of emotions and several sides to his personality. Robeson and Essie went to the United States to make the picture.

Although *The Emperor Jones* had an exotic jungle setting, the entire production was shot in a Long Island, New York, studio. It might have been possible to film part of it in the South, but Robeson had insisted in his contract that no work take place south of the Mason-Dixon Line where blacks faced discrimination. This was typical of how Robeson began to handle his film contracts. He set firm rules to try to maintain the dignity of blacks in his film scripts and on the movie set.

One obstacle Robeson could not overcome was the film censors who dictated changes in the film. To begin with, the New York Board of Censors objected that the actress Fredie Washington, who played Robeson's girlfriend in the film, looked too light-skinned to be a black. The censors insisted that some early scenes be reshot with her in dark makeup.

The producers also had to cut out a scene in which Brutus Jones strikes and kills a brutal white prison guard so that the actual action appears off camera. White Americans, the censors said, could not tolerate the idea of a black man killing a white.

In the fall of 1933, *The Emperor Jones* opened in theaters in New York. In Harlem, blacks flocked to see their hero, Paul Robeson, in the role that first won him fame on the stage. The Roosevelt Theater grossed more than $10,000 in the first week. Generally, reviewers rated the film very highly, but members of the black press objected because the film used the word "nigger" and because, they claimed, it perpetuated stereotypes about blacks as being morally corrupt and superstitious.

During Robeson's years in England, he and Essie had

developed a strong interest in Africa and African art. Like most American blacks, Robeson had known little about Africa, the land from which his slave ancestors came. But in England, he befriended many African students destined to become revolutionary leaders in their own lands, including Kwame Nkrumah, future president of Ghana, and Jomo Kenyatta of Kenya. He spent long hours talking to them at the West African Students Union, and the students made the Robesons honorary members of their group.

For many years, Europeans who had colonies in African nations had looked down on the art and culture of Africa as being crude and primitive. But early in the twentieth century, that view began to change. The pictures painted by Picasso and other artists of the Cubist movement often drew on African themes.

The Robesons were thrilled by this new recognition for African culture and took courses in African languages and anthropology. Paul Robeson wrote articles about African culture for British journals.

All this led naturally to his next film role in 1934. He readily accepted an offer to play the African chieftain Bosambo in the film *Sanders of the River,* a project of producer Alexander Korda and director Zoltan Korda.

Robeson began the film with great enthusiasm. At last a movie would go beyond the tired old scenes of blacks happily dancing on plantations or singing spirituals in church services. He believed that the film could help Americans understand Africa and help blacks reach out to the rich culture of their ancestors.

To add realism to the film, the Kordas sent a camera crew to Africa to visit tribes that had little contact with whites. Traveling over 15,000 miles, crew members shot miles and miles of film of natives in war, ceremonial, and fertility dances. Of this only about 2,000 feet was ever used. Some films were used to teach the dances to Robeson and Nina Mae McKinney, who played his wife.

As the production began, Robeson believed that a dignified, historically accurate film would be made about Africans. At a spot near Shepperton, England, just off the Thames River, the Kordas even built an African village of 150 conical roofed huts and kraals. Some 200 Africans, many of them workers on the English docks, were hired as actors and extras.

But Robeson's hopes for the film were crushed. When he saw the finished product, he found that Bosambo had been turned into a loyal subject of his colonial masters, a character with doglike devotion to Sanders and Great Britain. The changes, making the film favorable to British rule in Africa, took place during the editing process while Robeson was out of England on a trip. Robeson felt *Sanders of the River* betrayed the very people he was trying to help. He was determined never to let such a thing happen again.

At about the same time, another major event in his life would lead him to become an even more outspoken critic of imperialism in the black world and discrimination against blacks in America.

While Robeson was filming *Sanders of the River,* Sergey Eisenstein, the Russian film director, had become interested in doing a film on Toussaint L'Ouverture, the Haitian liberator and black leader. Eisenstein, famous for such films as *The Battleship Potemkin* and *October,* was impressed with the fact that L'Ouverture, a slave, one generation away from Africa, had raised an army to defeat Napoleon's troops. That fact alone reflected the genius of black people, Eisenstein felt.

Eisenstein had met Robeson some years before and sent his close friend, Marie Seton, to London. She invited Essie and Robeson to visit Moscow with her to discuss the film. At last, the Robesons decided, they would visit Russia, the country that had intrigued them for so long.

"I was not prepared for the endless friendliness"

It was in late December 1934 that Paul Robeson finally made the trip to Russia that he had dreamed of for many years. Besides studying Russian, he had regularly read the Soviet publications *Pravda* and *Isvestia*. He was particularly interested in what the Soviet government did in the Asian areas of Russia for minority groups—tribal people like the Yakuts and Uzbeks. Over the years, he had heard conflicting stories about life inside the Soviet Union. He had some doubts about the Russians, but he wanted to see the country for himself. So with Essie and Marie Seton, he boarded a train that traveled first to Germany and then to Russia.

Robeson had not visited Germany since 1930 when he appeared there in *The Emperor Jones*. In 1933, Adolf Hitler with his racist and anti-Jewish views had taken over the German government. His policies of hatred swept the country and became the guiding principles for most Germans. Even many who opposed Hitler's views did not resist.

When they arrived in Berlin, Robeson and the two women walked from the train station to the hotel where they planned on a one-day stay until their next train came in. Robeson called this brief stop "a day of horror—in an atmosphere of hatred, fear and suspicion."[1] On the streets, they sensed animosity and fear in the glances of others. Many people seemed stunned to see a black man walking openly on the sidewalks of Berlin. Everywhere the Robesons looked Nazi troopers were striding down the street in starched uniforms and driving sleek, official cars. When the Robesons and Seton finally reached the hotel, Paul Robeson threw himself on the bed. Strongly shaken by what he had seen, he did not want to leave the hotel again before their train left.

Soon after they arrived, Essie contacted a Jewish friend whom Robeson had met on his first visit to Germany. The friend came to their hotel and described the cloud of fear that hung over Jews and other dissenters in Nazi Germany. Already Hitler had removed all Jewish officials and any who had left-wing sympathies from civil service jobs. Jews were also barred from working in law, journalism, music, the theater, or radio. Earlier in the year in a bloody purge, Hitler had killed off dissenters among his followers. Some Jews had died as well. Yet just months before Robeson got to Germany, 38 million Germans, more than 90 percent of those voting, had given Hitler a yes vote of confidence.

For the rest of their stay in Germany, the Robesons and Seton ate in their hotel and went out only to watch a travelog at a nearby movie theater. There was a final moment of fear when the trio finally met their train. Essie went to handle the luggage, leaving Paul and Seton on the train platform. Then Robeson noticed that storm troopers, strong-arm paramilitary guards organized by the Nazi party, had lined up shoulder-to-shoulder, separating Robeson and Seton from other passengers on the platform. A passenger had evidently complained about seeing a white woman talking to a black man. The storm troopers began calling them names, and Robeson urged Marie Seton to get on the train. But she stuck close to him.

When Essie finally arrived, the little group was almost surrounded by the troopers. Robeson thought that the only way out was for him to let the men beat him up or for him to fight back. After all, he was taller than the tallest of the troops.

But rescue arrived as a locomotive chugged into the station. Robeson yelled at the women to board and he quickly climbed on, too. For a while it looked as if they might have to leave without their luggage, but at the last minute a porter threw their suitcases on the train.

Several hours passed before the Robesons and Marie Seton relaxed after this incident. As the train rolled out of Germany and into Poland, Robeson told his wife and friend: "I figured I could throw two of them onto the tracks and do some damage to two or three more before they got me down. I never understood what fascism was before."[2]

A final mix-up occurred at the Soviet border. Because the Robesons' passports were technically irregular, Russian customs officials were about to bar them from their country. Although it seems like an unbelievable story, Marie Seton claimed that the officials then took some of Robeson's records out of his bags and played them on a gramophone. They instantly recognized his voice, and when he sang a few bars, they were stunned to learn he was the man on the record. They quickly agreed to let him enter the country.

Robeson's attitude toward this trip has to be viewed in light of the political and economic climate in the United States in the 1930s. At the time many liberals in America and elsewhere had a rosier view of Russia than perhaps the facts warranted. They believed that Russia was the one country in the world striving for equality for all citizens. They also believed that Russia was the one country willing to oppose Hitler and Germany.

Just before this visit, Robeson had attended a seminar in London held by the League of Colored Peoples. Some speakers talked about how to achieve equality among different races, and one speech by an English dockworker impressed Robeson the most. The dockworker exclaimed that there was no need for seminars on ending inequality. Russia had all the answers. Just visit Russia and see how the Russians were doing, the speaker said.

At the same time, during the 1930s, American blacks were feeling the sharp bite of the Depression. Before economic hard times, whites had scorned domestic service—as maids and butlers and chauffeurs—and left those jobs for blacks because of their lower wages. But with high unemployment, whites started to take these jobs away from blacks.

So some disheartened American blacks migrated to Russia in hopes of finding better jobs. Among those doing so were Essie's brothers, John and Frank Goode. Some of these immigrants later regretted this move, but when the Robesons arrived in Russia, the promise of a new life seemed to shine brightly. At the Moscow train station, the Robesons met an exuberant group, including filmmaker Sergey Eisenstein and an American actor, Wayland Rudd, in Russia to appear in a film about blacks.

Although they came from very different cultures, Eisenstein and Robeson were about the same age and shared a strong love for the arts. They quickly became close friends. Eisenstein served supper for the Robesons in his room, which he had lit with candles in antique holders and furnished with chairs especially borrowed for the occasion. After dinner, he took them to see a Russian play, and then he sat up most of the night talking to Robeson about the evolution of foreign languages. Robeson also played African and Siamese records brought as a present for Eisenstein. Other all-night talks like this one were held again and again during the visit.

For the next two weeks, one party after another toasted the Robesons. On Christmas Eve, Eisenstein and the Robesons went to a festive dinner of turkey, caviar, and vodka at the country house of a top Soviet official. After dinner there was dancing and Robeson returned to Eisenstein's apartment to sing selections from the Russian opera by Mussorgsky, *Boris Godunov.* Another night, a banquet was held for the Robesons at the Dom Kino, the plush club house of cinema workers, where Robeson sang again from *Boris Godunov.* Afterward, the workers surged around him, pulling his hands and kissing him.

Another glittering reception was held by the All Union Society for Cultural Relations with Foreign Countries. The guests, including Russian artists, writers, and journalists, came in gowns and tuxedos. Some of them performed, and Robeson sang folk music. Later Robeson told a fellow American: "I have never faced an audience like the one the other night. They really know how to listen to music here, especially folk music."[3]

But Robeson wanted to find out how the workers lived in Russia and what he saw impressed him. "I was not prepared for the happiness I see on every face in Moscow," he told a reporter for an American Communist Party publication, the *Daily Worker,* during his visit. "I was aware that there was no starvation here, but I was not prepared for the bounding life; the feeling of safety and abundance and freedom that I find here, wherever I turn. I was not prepared for the endless friendliness, which surrounded me from the moment I crossed the border."[4]

When he talked to young people born since the Russian Revolution about discrimination against blacks in other countries, he said, they didn't seem to understand what he meant. And what he had read in U.S. newspapers about Russia didn't fit what he saw. He told a reporter: "Wherever I went I found plenty of food. Of course it wasn't in every case the finest food, but it was healthful and everyone got enough to eat. Besides those so-called backward peasants are learning all the latest dietary sciences in the preparation and selection of foods."[5]

The workers' homes seemed healthy and clean; the nurseries for children had the latest equipment; the factories had up-to-date machines; on the streetcars, men and women studied science and math books. There didn't seem to be any slums. "I visited the home of my brother-in-law (John Goode, working as a chauffeur in Moscow). His apartment had plenty of light, fresh air and space. Believe me he is very happy," Robeson said.[6]

Although many later criticized such statements, at the time of Robeson's visit Russia was having a small boost in its economy after lean years under its brutal leader Joseph Stalin. A few years before, Russia had suffered a severe famine in some areas as well as unrest among peasant farmers who didn't want to move to communal or collective farms. Some experts estimate that as many as 15 million people died in the upheaval caused by Stalin's Five Year Plan of economic development. But in 1934 and 1935, bountiful harvests meant that food rationing could gradually be abolished. Soviet factories were striving to meet production goals in order to compete in world markets. In 1932, in the depths of the Depression, for example, the Russians produced more steel than Germany, France, or Great Britain.

Everywhere Robeson went, on trams, buses, along the streets and parks, the Russians seemed interested in him and happy to meet him. "I was rested and buoyed up by the lovely, honest, wondering looks which did not see a Negro," he said.[7] "When Dad walked down the street," said Paul Robeson, Jr., "Russian kids would swarm all over him. It was inconceivable that something like that could happen in the United States at that time."[8]

Paul Robeson, Sr., believed that the various minority groups in Russia had achieved equality. Black, yellow, and white were treated in the same way. "In the minds of the masses there is not even the concept of a racial question," he told a reporter.[9]

What Robeson may not have known was that in Central Asia, shortly after the Soviet Revolution, many Moslem nomads had rebelled against the new Communist regime; tens of thousands were killed and thousands of others were forced off their land.

Robeson's visit to Russia was brief, and he actually saw little of the country. Robert Robinson, an American black who traveled to Russia in the 1930s to become a Soviet citizen, was also impressed with Russia when he first arrived. Later, after forty-four years, he left bitter and disillusioned. Although the Soviets claimed that they were not racially prejudiced, disdain for blacks lay beneath the surface in their minds, Robinson claimed. "I rarely met a Russian who thought blacks—or for that matter Orientals or any non-whites—were equal to him. Trying to deal with their prejudice was like a phantom," Robinson said.[10]

Robinson claimed that almost every black who became a Soviet citizen in the early 1930s disappeared from Moscow within seven years. The lucky ones returned home. Some went into exile in Siberian prison camps. Others were executed.

All this lay in the future, and during his visit, Robeson could only draw quick conclusions. But the trip awakened his interest in Marxism and communism, which he saw as tools to aid other developing nations. He saw Russia as the world's strongest foe of the Nazis. "I believe that the Soviet Union is the bulwark of civilization against both war and fascism. I think it has the most brilliant and sincere peace policy in the world today."[11]

Robeson left Russia promising to return to make Eisenstein's movie. He had hopes for many new projects involving Russia, perhaps a folk song tour and a visit to the minorities of East Russia to study their music. Over and over, he told friends and relatives and reporters that he wanted to go back.

"For freedom and against the new slavery"

But the film with Russia's Sergey Eisenstein was never meant to be. Over the next few years, Robeson and then Eisenstein were tied up in work that kept them from collaborating.

Back in England, Robeson appeared in May 1935 in *Stevedore* in London. Originally produced in the United States, the play was about a militant black dockworker, framed by a criminal mob. Critics gave the play mixed notices although Robeson won compliments. Once again, he had found a drama with a strong message, but it failed to make money.

For the next several years, Robeson made film after film for big studios, each time struggling to find roles and stories portraying blacks in a fresh and honest way. Sometimes he came close to his goal, while at other times he failed. But like no other black actor before him, he put demands on Hollywood moviemakers about the kinds of films he wanted and his salary and working conditions.

After his wildly successful run in *Show Boat*, the play's producers wanted him to play the lead in the film of the musical. The Robesons hesitated to leave Europe to make the movie, and Essie wrote to Universal films to ask such a high salary that they were sure Robeson wouldn't get the part. But Universal agreed, and in the fall of 1935, the couple left for Hollywood. During the trip, they got to see Pauli, who had attended school in Canada while the Robesons traveled in Russia and worked in Europe.

The movie of *Show Boat* was a smash hit, and newspaper critics praised Robeson's singing and complained that his part should have been bigger. Black newspapers, however, criticized the role. One paper even said Robeson did "a better job of portraying the Negro man as a shiftless moron than he did as a weak-kneed prince in *Sanders of the River.*"[1] Robeson understood this criticism. Throughout this time, he had also continued his studies of Africa and black culture and he was studying Marxism and socialism in greater depth.

The Communist *The Daily Worker* sharply questioned why he appeared in such films as *Sanders of the River.* The paper's reporter, Benjamin Davis, Jr., who became a close friend of Robeson's, called the film "an out and out betrayal of the African colonials." He told Robeson that he had become the tool of British imperialism in the movie.

"You're right," Robeson replied, "and I think all the attacks against me and the film were correct. I was roped into the picture because I wanted to portray the culture of the African people in which I have the greatest interest."[2]

The conversation reflected Robeson's developing political opinions. More and more, he recognized that his fame made him a representative of black people worldwide. He could not betray these people by working in artistic projects that demeaned blacks. He had also begun to take positive action on behalf of blacks and Africa and endorsed a number of black and left-wing political groups.

When the Robesons returned to England after *Show Boat*, Essie decided to visit the Africa that she and Paul had read about and studied for so long. For some years, she had been troubled by the opinions of Europeans and other

(69)

whites who had lived in Africa and who claimed that African blacks had primitive minds that could not grasp Western ideas. She was sure that the many Africans she had met in Europe had the same ideas and ambitions as she did. She and Paul had also been upset when six-year-old Pauli, on a film set for *Sanders of the River*, had been surprised to see all the Africans. "Why, there are lots of brown people," he had said. "Lots of black people too; we're not the only ones."[3] Suddenly, the Robesons realized that from baby-hood on, Pauli had lived in an almost all-white world. The only blacks he had seen were his parents and grandmother, Robeson's accompanist Lawrence Brown, and some visitors to their home. Essie felt that she should show Pauli that a whole continent was filled with millions of black and brown people. Robeson wanted to go along, but his film career was taking off. He had two years' worth of jobs ahead.

It was a major adventure in the 1930s for a young mother like Essie and her small child to set off for Africa. Essie embarked on weeks of vaccinations and injections and purchases of special gear. Although she had arranged many trips before, she faced many obstacles when she sought visas for African colonies of European nations. She con-cluded that racial discrimination was involved. "It seems if you are Negro, you can't make up your mind to go to Africa and just go. . . . The white people in Africa do not want educated Negroes traveling around seeing how their brothers live."[4] But finally in May 1936, she and Pauli kissed Robeson goodbye at London's Waterloo Station. As they parted, Robeson promised to work on problems that Essie still had with visas. "He is such a dear person," she wrote later. "It was a wrench to leave him."[5]

After she left, Paul worked on a film produced by a British company, *The Song of Freedom*. Documentary scenes for the film were shot in West Africa, and Robeson insisted that he have a contract that allowed him an editing role, to avoid the sad experiences he had with *Sanders of the River*. At a press conference, Robeson described *The Song of Freedom* as the "first film to give a true picture of many aspects of the life of the colored man in the West. Hitherto on the screen, he has been caricatured or presented only as a comedy character. This film shows him as a real man."[6] Robeson may have viewed his new movie as a step forward, but it wasn't a box office success.

Soon after Essie and Pauli came home in August, Robeson began work on *King Solomon's Mines*, based on the novel by H. Rider Haggard. Cedric Hardwicke, who had appeared with Robeson in *Show Boat* in London, played the lead, Allan Quartermaine, a white explorer who travels to what is now Zimbabwe to search for the mines of King Solomon. Paul played Umbopas, chief of an African tribe, who guides Quartermaine to the mines in hopes of regaining a kingdom stolen from him.

The film, done largely in England, but with some scenes of Africa cut into it, was designed to show off Robeson's powerful voice and featured several songs. Robeson was excited about the role because of the fame of the novel. But for the most part, the natives in the film were portrayed as ignorant and gullible, prone to the use of magic and witchcraft. Reviews again were not strong, and most critics thought of the movie as an adventure story aimed at children.

With his latest film completed, the Robesons traveled to the Soviet Union again. During the trip, Robeson, accompanied by Lawrence Brown, gave a concert tour sponsored by the Moscow State Philharmonic. They arrived in Russia just after dictator Stalin had led a special commission in rewriting the Soviet constitution to make it more "democratic." The Soviets evidently showed Paul this document, and he praised it warmly in a radio broadcast, calling it a "historic new charter of the rights of man."[7]

Provisions that spelled out equality for all races and nationalities especially impressed Robeson. Every citizen at age eighteen could vote directly for representatives to Russia's supreme council. Balloting for the first time was to be secret. The only problem was that only the Communist Party members could pick the candidates.

During this visit by the Robesons, the nation was also engulfed in a series of widely publicized purges in which Stalin put on trial party leaders whom he wanted eliminated. Many of those forced to confess and later executed or sent to Siberia were former heroes of the Russian Revolution. The first such trial was held in August 1936, a few months before Robeson's arrival. Another took place in January 1937 during Robeson's visit. Many other Russians were tried in secret, and some experts estimate that at least 7 million people were imprisoned or executed in the process.

Around the world, many people sympathetic to the Soviets and to communism were horrified by the trials. Some broke forever with the Communist Party. Even so, many Americans insisted that the trials were needed to maintain the purity of Russia's revolutionary ideals. Many sympathizers with Russia also believed that Stalin was fighting against fascist forces inside Russia, the same kind of fascists who were gaining strength in Germany.

The Robesons shared some of these views. In a book that Essie wrote several years later with author Pearl Buck, she said that Soviet leaders had first tried to convert their foes and then tried to persuade them to cooperate. "When they not only would not co-operate, but deliberately worked against the government, they were 'removed.' If the government was to survive, it had to remove them."[8]

In Moscow, Robeson attended an orchestra concert at the Bolshoi Theater where everyone stood to applaud and cheer Stalin, and Robeson did the same with tears flowing down his face. He lifted up his son, Pauli, to wave to Joseph Stalin.

Robeson never openly spoke out against Stalin, said his son, because he saw the Soviet Union as "a counterweight to Western imperialism." It was a country with faults, but it opposed the Western nations that insisted on dominating and exploiting colonies in Africa and Asia. "He believed that Russia made the third world independence movement possible and made colonial freedom possible," Paul Robeson, Jr., said. "He felt that you don't criticize a friend over internal problems."9

The Robesons traveled from Leningrad, near the Arctic Circle, to Moscow and Kiev and on to Odessa on the Black Sea. Everywhere Paul Robeson sang, Soviet workers packed his concerts. He felt more than ever a bond between the Soviet people and blacks. Soviet audiences seemed far closer to folk traditions than those in America. In one concert in Odessa, a listener was so swept up by Robeson's rich and mellow voice that he jumped on stage, kissed Robeson, and pinned on his coat a button bearing a picture of Lenin, the leader of the Russian Revolution.

While in Russia, Paul and Essie Robeson made a momentous decision. One day, while Pauli had been playing in London with other children, a mother had snatched her child away from him out of fear because he was a black. The mother made a racist statement that shocked Robeson. Now Robeson decided that to avoid repeating such experiences Pauli should go to school in Russia where Robeson had seen no prejudice, no racism.

The decision wasn't made lightly. Essie Robeson even contacted some American Communists, Eugene and Peggy Dennis, living in Russia to ask them what they thought about the idea. Eugene Dennis told Essie to publicize their plan widely and to be sure to arrange that they could take Pauli home whenever they wished. Pauli was enrolled after he became more fluent in Russian, but Robeson told the press that he still wanted his son to visit America often to learn U.S. traditions.

Moving to the Soviet Union was not a difficult adjustment for Pauli Robeson. He had already lived in a number of different countries, and as usual his grandmother accompanied him to Russia as she had to all the other places where he had attended school. He became fluent in Russian within six weeks. Sending Pauli to school in Moscow meant that the Robesons would visit Russia again and again in the next few years during Pauli's school vacations and holidays.

In these last years before World War II, the nightmare of fascism grew more horrifying. Like many liberals, the Robesons were particularly shaken when civil war broke out in Spain. The Spanish Loyalists were fighting the forces of Generalissimo Franco, who was receiving aid from Germany and the fascists.

The rise of Nazi power in Europe made Paul Robeson think about the United States and what it meant to him. He began to see the struggles of blacks in the United States as part of the worldwide fight against fascism. He wanted to speak out as never before about the cause of Spain, about the crusade against the Nazis, and about his growing allegiance to socialism.

He yearned to return to the United States to serve as an activist for his people. In a radio broadcast from the Soviet Union before he left, he urged blacks and all "lovers of peace" to line up behind "those forces which are leading the struggle for peace and against war, for collective security and against wars of aggression, for freedom and against the new slavery."[10]

"Am I an American?"

Back in England, Paul Robeson appeared next in the film *Big Fella*, written by the black writer Claude McKay. In the story set in Marseilles, France, Robeson played a dockworker, Banjo. What Robeson liked about the role was that Banjo survived in an integrated society and was strong physically and mentally. Lawrence Brown had a small role and Essie also had a part that won her good reviews.

Another film project that year, *Jericho*, disappointed many critics because it had a weak story line and because Robeson was once again in a movie set in Africa. Robeson liked the way the film portrayed war and Africa. He was also allowed to change the end of the movie to make it more realistic. But he had grown discouraged about the parts the film industry kept offering him. "I thought I could do something for the Negro race on the films; show the truth about them—and about other people too," he told a reporter for the Communist paper *The London Daily Worker* as his two films were being finished up. "I used to do my part and go away feeling satisfied. Thought everything was O.K. Well, it wasn't. Things were twisted and changed—distorted. They didn't mean the same."[1]

He announced that he wouldn't do any more films for major commercial companies, although he did make one more big studio film, *Tales of Manhattan,* in 1942. He wanted to stick to small independent filmmakers who would give him what he called "cast-iron" parts, roles that wouldn't change during shooting or editing. More and more, he became convinced that he could act and sing only for working people. He announced that he would put a limit of five shillings a head on tickets for his future concerts.

Meanwhile, Robeson spent more time in political activities. In 1937, he helped found the Council on African Affairs, formed to aid colonies in Africa in their efforts to win freedom and independence. This group went on to become a pioneering influence in the civil rights movement in the United States as well as aiding the Pan Africanist movement. The group set up an African library and a collection of African art and put out a monthly newsletter of Africa. Money was also raised to feed hungry Africans.

But it was more than a humanitarian and cultural group. For almost twenty years, the council served as the strongest force in the United States working to help Africans achieve independence. It represented one of Robeson's greatest achievements on behalf of freedom and justice as it organized early campaigns against apartheid in South Africa, supported jailed resistance leaders in Africa, and launched protests against lynching and other injustices in the United States.

Co-founders with Robeson were Max Yergan, a black YMCA secretary, and Alphaeus Hunton, a professor at Howard University. Among the group's major financial supporters was Frederick V. Field, of the Chicago department-store family. Later, when United States officials denounced the council as a subversive group, Robeson and Yergan became political enemies.

During the 1930s Robeson also sang in many concerts to raise funds for the Spanish Republican forces, but just raising money was not enough for him. In January 1938,

Robeson and Essie went to Spain where he sang on the frontlines and in hospitals for troops of the International Brigade, including soldiers of many nations who were fighting Franco. The Spanish opened their arms to him; everywhere he went, they called him Pablito. Robeson even played football with a group of boys in a zone of Madrid being bombarded by artillery. For one of his performances on the fighting lines in Teruel, the guns on both sides fell silent while Robeson's voice rang out in an open-air concert.

Returning to London, Robeson announced that he would produce a film in which he would play Oliver Law, a black leader from the International Brigade, who died in battle in the Spanish Civil War. The film was never made. But Robeson did appear in one of those movies by small independent companies that he had said he wanted to pursue. This time the film was *Proud Valley*, produced by Ealing Studios and focusing on the harsh life of coal miners in Wales. Robeson played David Goliath, a mine worker–organizer based on a true-to-life black American who had worked on the docks in England and then later in the mines.

By the time the war had ended in Spain with Franco as victor, Robeson was back home in the United States to appear in a Broadway drama, *John Henry.* Robeson and Essie, Pauli, and Essie's mother rented an apartment in New York. Several months later, they bought an estate in Enfield, Connecticut, called "The Beeches." The stately home, complete with swimming pool, tennis court, and bowling alley, stood on two-and-a-half acres of land set with towering trees. With its tall massive columns, the house resembled a colonial plantation mansion.

Before the purchase, Essie had the bank poll the neighbors to make sure they would not object to having a black family live nearby. It was a home that Essie treasured. Once they moved in, she enrolled in a local school to work on her Ph.D. During these years, Robeson's relationship with his son, Pauli, grew closer. "We were partners in sports and intellectual things," said Paul, Jr. "He was always asking me questions about the connections between things. He helped open up my mind."[2]

During the summer of 1939, Robeson was interviewed after his return to America, and he poured out his soul over what his country meant to him. At age forty-one, he seemed to have mellowed and matured. He no longer felt isolated in the United States; he felt a new feeling of peace. When bigots were cruel to him, he no longer lashed out in anger. He had decided that this racism was the result of ignorance rather than malice.

On the first day of his return, he was invited to a tea party at one of New York's finest hotels. When he approached the front elevator, he was told to use the freight elevator instead. "Several years back I would have smarted at this insult and carried the hurt for a long time," Robeson said. "Now—no—I was just amused and explained to the elevator boy that I didn't belong with the freight, that as I was the guest of honor at the tea, my hosts might be surprised to see me arrive with the supplies. The elevator man caught the idea very quickly."[3]

This was a far different Robeson from the college student who had been ready to kill his attacker on the football field or the performer who preferred to live in England rather than endure the insults of waiters and hotel clerks in the United States. That didn't mean he wasn't fighting racism and discrimination. But not only were blacks the victims, Robeson said, there was oppression as well for Jews and Chinese and for working people all over the world. "I found that where forces have been the same, whether people weave, build, pick cotton, or dig in the mines, they understand each other in the common language of work, suffering and protest," he said.[4]

This growing love for his country and new kinship for

working people make it easy to understand why one of his next projects was such a success. In October 1939, a young radio producer approached him about singing a patriotic song on a new radio show, *The Pursuit of Happiness*, on the Columbia Broadcasting System. The song was based on a poem, "The Ballad of Uncle Sam," by a Virginia poet, John Latouche, who wrote it as a statement against intolerance and persecution. Then a composer, Earl Robinson, set the poem to music and it was renamed by the show's producer, Norman Corwin, as "Ballad for Americans."

Originally, CBS had wanted to hire Robeson for the radio show, but network officials thought his fee was too high. Then they heard the ballad, and they knew it was meant for Robeson, regardless of the cost. Robeson and the composer met several times to rehearse and adjust the music to Robeson's voice.

Finally, on November 5, the program host, Burgess Meredith, introduced the ballad with these words:

"Democracy is a good thing. It works. It may creak a bit, but it works. And in its working, it still turns out good times, good news, good people. . . . Life, liberty and the pursuit of happiness—of these we sing!"[5]

For eleven minutes, while Earl Robinson's American People's Chorus sang behind him, Robeson's baritone rang out with the words that summed up many of his political feelings. It was a song that reached the American people at precisely the right moment. Just two months before, Hitler had invaded Poland and World War II had begun in Europe. Americans knew that they would probably have to enter the fight themselves within a short time. Robeson's song expressed exactly what they felt about their country, about their nation's need to bind together in unity to face the Nazi foe. Not only that, the singer was a black man, part of a race that had been oppressed for centuries, but who was expressing his allegiance to his country with a powerful voice.

For two minutes, the studio audience burst into applause and stamped their feet and shouted while the show was still on the air. For fifteen minutes afterward, audience members continued to applaud. Calls from hundreds of patriotic Americans jammed the CBS switchboards in New York and in Hollywood. For the next few days, letters poured in asking for the words and music to the ballad. Robeson and the American People's Chorus sang the ballad again and again in performances over the next few months, and he recorded the song for Victor Records.

If Americans had forgotten about Paul Robeson during his years in Europe, they awoke to his talents as never before. He was interviewed again and again about his political views. *Collier's* magazine named him the nation's "favorite male Negro singer" and "America's No. 1 Negro entertainer."

During the winter of 1940, Robeson and Lawrence Brown made their most successful nationwide concert tour to date. Although they sometimes crossed into the Southern states to perform, Robeson would not sing where blacks and whites could not sit together. He performed the black spirituals that had made him famous, but he also sang Russian and Mexican folk music, the Hebrew Kaddish, and numbers by Beethoven, Mussorgsky and Mendelssohn. And of course, the audiences wanted to hear "Ballad for Americans." In July 1940 he sang the "Ballad" before an audience of 30,000 at the Hollywood Bowl in Los Angeles. Another 160,000 packed Grant Park in Chicago to hear him sing.

But while he had won the hearts of his countrymen, almost from the first days of his arrival in the United States, Robeson raised questions in their minds with some of his statements and political stands. Some of his controversial opinions involved Soviet Russia during the early days of the war.

Shortly after the Germans had invaded Poland from the West, the Soviets had invaded from the East. It was later learned that Stalin had signed a secret pact with Germany dividing up much of Eastern Europe. The pact shocked Western leaders, and many Communists in the United States quit the party and renounced Stalin and Russia.

Then Russia pressured the Baltic countries to admit Soviet troops who were supposed to protect them. Estonia, Latvia, and Lithuania were eventually swallowed up by Russia. When Russia tried the same thing with Finland, the Finns resisted and held off the Soviets for several months. But in March 1940, Finland had to give up much of her territory for a naval base. The Finnish situation outraged many American liberals. Others claimed that the press was trumping up a case against the Soviets. Robeson was among those who doubted that Russia was totally at fault in the invasion. Surely Finland provoked the attack?

The Herbert Hoover Relief Fund soon announced a plan to raise funds for the Finns by putting on a theatrical benefit in New York. Robeson was asked to perform, but he refused. The newspapers questioned his decision and asked what his relationship was to Russia. After all, hadn't his son gone to school in Moscow? "Robeson," said the Associated Press, ". . . said he was not personally a Communist."6

In 1941, just before the attack on Pearl Harbor, Robeson appeared for unions and labor groups. He was active in the Committee to Aid China and the Joint Anti-Fascist Refugee Committee. In September, he even appeared at a mass meeting at Madison Square Garden in New York organized to appeal for freedom for Earl Browder, a U.S. Communist leader who was imprisoned in 1940 for passport irregularities. "I am here tonight," Robeson said, "because I know that you know that there can be no more honest evidence of a sincere decision to defeat fascism along with the sending of tanks and every possible aid to the Soviet Union, than the freeing of Earl Browder. . . ."7 Paul Robeson would continue his political activities over the next few years, but soon his attention focused on a new artistic goal.

"Did you ever know such luck as I have?"

In December 1941, the Japanese attacked Pearl Harbor, and the United States was thrust into World War II. Russia, feared by many Americans since the Communist Revolution, was now the ally of the United States. Suddenly, Robeson's opinions about the Russians no longer seemed so radical and strange any more.

After the war began, Robeson continued his activities for unions, but he also performed at War Bond rallies and toured weapons factories to sing for workers. He gave free concerts for aid to black soldiers and to China and Russia.

Beginning in 1942, he faced one of the greatest artistic challenges of his career. He wanted to try Othello again; he felt he knew more about the part than he had in the first production; he wanted to play the role as it had never been played before. One young woman was probably more responsible than anyone else for helping Robeson in this. She was Margaret Webster, the daughter of British actress May Whitty. A well-known Shakespearean director, Webster had watched Robeson in his first production of *Othello,* and then in 1938, Robeson had talked to her about putting on a new production.

Due to Robeson's busy schedule, they could not work on the project until 1942. The first difficulty was finding someone to play Desdemona. "It had been all right, they said, for Peggy Ashcroft to do it in London, but she was English and that was London. In America—a white girl play love scenes with a black man . . . they were appalled," Webster said.[1] At last Webster signed a new young actress, Uta Hagen, to play Desdemona. Her husband, José Ferrer, would play Iago.

The second hurdle was finding a summer stock theater where the play could try out before moving to Broadway. Webster finally signed the Brattle Theater in Cambridge, Massachusetts, close to Boston and Harvard.

Webster found Robeson was difficult to direct. His voice and appearance were overpowering, she said. With his fine mind, he appreciated poems and verse. But she complained that he spoke artificially, like an opera singer or a very serious preacher. His love scenes were beautiful and tender, but he could never show the violent anger and jealousy that the play demanded.

While Robeson as Othello stood solid and immobile on stage, the smaller, quicker Ferrer danced around him energetically. Robeson later told an interviewer: "The way I play it, I'm calm, I'm quiet, through all the early part. I don't make an unnecessary move. And I think that's right. Of course, if I didn't have a mighty active Iago, I couldn't get away with that massive calmness, perhaps, but with Joe (José Ferrer) all over the stage the way he is, it is an effective contrast."[2]

On top of it all, during rehearsals, Webster had to constantly defend to the press her decision that Shakespeare meant a black, and not a white man or an Arab, to play Othello. "I did this with conviction because I myself believe it. But I found that you could make a perfectly good case for anything you wanted to prove," she said.[3]

The production opened one steamy August evening in 1942. The Brattle Theater's four hundred seats were packed and other audience members stood around the walls. Hundreds of others tried and failed to buy tickets. Backstage, perspiration poured off the players who were sweltering in velvet gowns and cloaks and high leather boots. But it wasn't just the heat, it was tension and nervousness that made them feel hot and flushed.

Once the curtain rose, the audience sat quietly in their seats for four hours without coughing or moving around or rattling programs. When the last scene was played, the audience thundered its approval with cheers and claps and pounded on the floor with their feet, a traditional salute at Harvard.

The Harvard and Boston newspapers were overwhelming in their praise. Whatever Robeson's faults, his incredible voice and his powerful presence on stage overwhelmed them. "The beautiful sonority of his speaking voice, the dignity of his bearing, his believable transformation from the kindliest of husbands, a man wracked by the overwhelming passion of jealousy, makes the multiple murders of *Othello* bring to that final scene of death not just nobility but understanding."[4]

The next day, the phones rang wildly with offers from Broadway investors who wanted to help finance the show, the play that they had all been turning down just a short time before.

Over the next few months, the play moved on to other theaters outside New York, including Princeton, New Jersey, Robeson's birthplace, and Boston, Philadelphia, and New Haven. Critics applauded, but they were not unanimous in praise. Some said Robeson did not follow through on the wonderful opening night, and others said that he was too studied and self-conscious, that his performance lacked spontaneity.

Meanwhile, the cast prepared for the opening in New York. The production stage manager, Robeson, and Webster ran the operation. New sets were designed, creating a series of palace rooms and walled-in streets. Robeson was to wear costumes that shimmered with metallic thread and a blood-red cloak that trailed from his shoulder. To get ready, he also had to lose thirty pounds.

What happened on opening night, October 19, 1943, at the Shubert Theater was more than just a theatrical triumph, it was a dramatic moment in American history and in black history. And for Paul Robeson it fulfilled one of his greatest dreams.

Moments after the actors and actresses walked on stage, the tension leaped like a spark between cast and audience. When the curtain finally came down, the main characters who lay "dead" on stage all had tears running down their faces. For twenty minutes the audience applauded its thanks and called for speeches from cast members who found themselves unable to say a word. It was a triumphant opening, but not because Robeson was a fine actor, Webster said. She continued to look dimly on his acting talents. But, she said, something else about him meant that his performance "matched the part and the hour. From the moment he walked onto the stage and said, very quietly, 'Tis better as it is,' he endowed the play with a stature and perspective which I have not seen before or since."[5]

Robeson had chosen to do a play that spoke about the question of relationships between blacks and whites, by the greatest playwright who ever lived, at a time when Americans were looking for new answers to questions about racial discrimination.

The next morning, the papers tossed adjective after adjective of praise at the play and a long line formed to buy tickets. There was some criticism, of course. One critic complained that Robeson "makes no use of his body, which becomes a dead weight."[6]

Robeson was staying with friends when the play opened

and the morning after he jubilantly read reviews in all the New York papers. "Boy, I'm lucky," he told his friends. "Did you ever know such luck as I have."[7]

Often in the past, he had tired of acting in the same play night after night, repeating his lines until he could recite them backward as well as forward. But this time he felt absorbed in the role and saw a meaning to his being in the theater. "Through my performance of Othello I have been able to reach people who would never listen to me if I was in some other field."[8] And he was reaching people: professors, students, soldiers, actors, musicians, housepainters, millionaires, society matrons. People who had never seen Shakespeare performed before, who had no idea what *Othello* was about, went to see Robeson.

Halfway through the run, a *New York Herald Tribune* editorial said it was too bad that the United States had to consider it noteworthy that a black man should play Othello. "But it is surely a recognition of the essential folly of such group antagonisms," the paper said, "a sign of hope for the future—when a Negro actor of the quality of Mr. Robeson is so enthusiastically welcomed into the great tradition of the English-speaking stage in a part of such power and nobility."[9]

Honors poured in for Robeson. Seven thousand people, including many famous names, attended his forty-sixth birthday party, an event put on by the Council on African Affairs at an armory in New York City. Just before the play closed in June 1944, the American Academy of Arts and Letters gave him its diction award, an honor previously won by only nine other actors and actresses.

By the end of the New York run, *Othello* had set new records for Shakespeare on Broadway with 296 performances and 494,839 paid admissions. In spite of these records, Webster did not always find Robeson easy to work with. He could be stubborn and demanding. "If there was anything he wanted done, or not done, he flexed those muscles—more plainly, he just said he would not play the following performance, or any other, unless he got what he wanted," she said.[10]

Still, most of the time his demands were small things, and often they were favors and privileges he wanted for other cast members instead of himself. Sometimes he offended Webster without realizing what he was doing. At one point, he arranged with a recording company to record the play without letting her know about it.

Throughout the run, Robeson carried on his political activities and often dashed from meetings to the stage with only minutes to spare. Webster grew upset and told him that one of the theater's greatest roles ever deserved more concentration. But he was always apologetic later. "It was hard to get—or to stay—angry with Paul," Webster said.[11]

When he was a youngster, Robeson's relatives and friends had always told him he was special, that he was meant for greatness. Certainly, at a young age he had reached many high goals, and his talents had won money and fame for him in the entertainment world. But it was nothing compared to the respect and renown he received after *Othello*. To whites, he represented someone who had reached the top in their world in spite of the obstacles of racial discrimination. He had proved it could be done.

After a brief rest, the cast took *Othello* on a cross-country forty-five-city tour that lasted several months. The cast would not perform in any theater where there was discrimination against blacks. So most Southern states were barred from the tour.

"I am not a Communist"

The scene was a three-day youth meeting in Columbia, South Carolina, in mid-October 1946. Some nine hundred young people poured into town to hear Southern black leaders speak, but most of all to listen to Paul Robeson and W. E. B. Du Bois, then editor of a publication of the National Association for the Advancement of Colored People. Although Communist Party members from the Southern Negro Youth Congress had helped organize the event, most of those attending were blacks with no party connection, young people hoping to end discrimination and racial bias.

After small group meetings, the peak moment arrived Saturday night when a crowd mobbed Columbia's city auditorium. After introductions, Paul Robeson, tall and dignified, took the microphone to speak for the need to change life in the South, the need to stamp out racism throughout the nation. His powerful voice rolled across the auditorium in a massive wave sweeping over the hearts of his listeners.

Then came the songs: "A Balm in Gilead" and "Jacob's Ladder." Finally the whole audience joined in on James Weldon Johnson's Negro National Anthem as Robeson's baritone thundered over their voices. Afterward, some people from the conference were invited to meet Robeson and the other speakers at a reception at a local black university.

When the door to the reception room opened and Robeson appeared, many in the crowd rushed up to talk to him.

In the 1940s, Paul Robeson attended meeting after meeting like the one in Columbia. Gradually, his political life consumed his career, and more and more he performed at rallies and protest meetings and fund-raisers. Often he appeared before groups in which Communist party members were involved. He was not interested in what label other people had or what organizations they belonged to so long as they fought for a good cause and believed in justice for all. He became more than a famous entertainer, he became a spokesman for blacks and for workers. To them, he was a leader who did not compromise his ideals for money, a fighter who battled to get a fair deal for all races. But not everyone looked up to Paul Robeson. Many whites and government officials were uncomfortable with his message. He challenged the values on which they had built their world.

Many causes that Robeson adopted during World War II and shortly after were principles that most Americans now favor wholeheartedly. He opposed imperialism, the continuing domination of small or poor countries by other wealthier countries. He pushed for racial integration in America's armed forces. He demanded an end to the lynching of blacks by mobs of lawless whites in the Southern states. These ideas were endorsed by liberal political groups at the time, including the Communist party. Measures to correct these problems and to end these outrages eventually became law in the United States. But in the 1940s, Robeson marched ahead of the times.

"I have often been asked," Robeson said, " 'Paul, are you doing right by being so outspoken in these times of hysteria?' And: 'Wouldn't you be of greater service to the race if you just devoted yourself to being an artist and didn't make those speeches which get the white folks so upset?' "[1]

In late 1943, Kenesaw Mountain Landis, the first commissioner of major league baseball, and other baseball officials gathered at a New York City hotel. Robeson led a delegation of black newspaper executives to the meeting to plead that black players be allowed to play professional baseball as he had once played professional football. Compared to the strong language of civil rights activists of the future, Robeson sounded almost apologetic. "I can understand the owners' fears that there would be trouble if Negroes were to play in the big leagues, but my football experience showed me such fears are groundless," he said. "Because baseball is a national game, it is up to baseball to see that discrimination does not become the American pattern."[2]

Landis and other baseball officials agreed there was no reason why blacks couldn't play in the major leagues, but it wasn't until 1947 that a black player, Jackie Robinson, wore a Brooklyn Dodgers uniform.

As World War II ended, representatives of the stronger nations met to plan how the world would be run once peace came. Among the questions to be answered was who would control the colonies in Africa and Asia that had once been run by France and Germany and other European countries? Robeson and his Council on African Affairs held a conference on that issue in New York in April 1944. They wanted to impress on government officials that African countries and other colonies must have independence.

During these years, Robeson befriended many controversial people, some of whom had problems with the federal government. In pressing to get blacks into baseball, for example, Robeson worked side by side with an active Communist, Benjamin Davis. Robeson had first met him in Harlem many years before when both were fresh out of college and headed for law careers. Davis joined the Communist party and became the editor of some Communist publications. Then he was elected to the New York City Council in 1943. Eventually, Davis was arrested and prosecuted for his connections with Communists.

Another friend was Harry Bridges, a San Francisco dockworker, who organized the International Longshoremen's and Warehousemen's Union. Bridges, born in Australia, was ordered deported as a Communist in 1939 and spent many years fighting to stay in the United States. In 1943, he made Robeson an honorary lifetime member of his union. Robeson's ties also deepened with the black scholar and writer, W. E. B. Du Bois, and he sang at several birthday dinners for Du Bois.

Although Robeson and his friends and their crusades may have aroused controversy during World War II, it wasn't until after the war that serious conflicts arose. Robeson contended that his ideas never changed, it was just that the political climate grew chillier, particularly about Communism and the Soviet Union.

During the war the Soviet Union was allied with the United States. But when peace came in 1945, the United States began to look fearfully at Russia's growing influence in Eastern Europe. U.S. officials were also terrified that the Soviet Union might learn how to make America's powerful new weapon, the atom bomb, recently dropped on Japan. Eventually, the Russians did make a bomb, and many Americans were sure that spies had given away their precious atomic secrets.

But Robeson saw it differently and believed that the United States should continue its friendship with Russia. Two years before the war ended, he received an honorary degree from Morehouse College in Atlanta, Georgia. In his acceptance speech he praised the strides made by the Soviet Union in training people once thought backward.

Two years later, Robeson made a similar speech as he accepted the Spingarn Medal, an annual award of the

NAACP. The awards ceremony was held at the Biltmore Hotel in New York before an audience of several hundred people. The medal honored his achievements in the theater and in concerts as well as his stands for human rights. But according to a black newspaper which reported on the event, Robeson "shocked" the audience by his sympathetic statements about the Soviet Union. In Russia, Robeson said, "Full employment is a fact, and not a myth, and discrimination is non-existent."[3]

All the while, Robeson continued his concerts for huge audiences. In 1945–46, he did one hundred and fifteen of them and also took a five-week concert tour of Europe once peace was declared. The following year he did eighty-five more concerts.

But politics intruded more and more into his performing career. In mid-1946, Robeson threw himself into a crusade to end lynchings in the South, a fight that ended with his own political beliefs in the spotlight. First, Robeson appeared at a rally in New York's Madison Square Garden with Henry A. Wallace, secretary of commerce under President Truman. As one of the evening's speakers, Robeson condemned lynchings. Wallace's differences with the Truman administration had grown, particularly in regard to Truman's get-tough policies with Russia. In September, Wallace was forced to resign his post.

At about the same time, Robeson became chairman of the Crusade Against Lynching, which launched a one-hundred-day effort against mob violence. The crusade began with a rally at a Chicago church attended by about 1,500 delegates.

Then Robeson and Mrs. Harper Sibley, president of the United Council of Church Women, and several others visited Truman on the morning of September 23. Robeson asked the president to formally oppose lynching. He noted that the timing would be appropriate because on September

22, 1862, Abraham Lincoln had issued a proclamation freeing the slaves. Robeson also urged Truman to recommend that Congress pass an anti-lynching bill.

Although Truman said he disapproved of lynching, his attitude was cool. Perhaps Robeson's support for Wallace played a role in the visit. Truman became especially angry when Mrs. Sibley asked him how the United States could, in good conscience, try the Nazi officials for their war crimes when U.S. officials allowed lynchings to continue.

At that point, Truman heatedly objected that loyal Americans should not confuse domestic problems like lynching with U.S. foreign policy. Robeson warned Truman that returning black veterans were growing restless and wanted the justice they had fought for in World War II. The situation might end in a federal emergency, Robeson said. Blacks might take action, he said.

Robeson had gone too far with the sometimes hot-headed Truman. The red-faced president shook his fist at Robeson and objected that he was being threatened. The session ended uncomfortably with Truman refusing to take any action. As the group left the meeting, members were swamped by newspaper reporters demanding to know what had happened. Then they asked Robeson a key question, one that was coming up again and again in the growing Cold War atmosphere following World War II: Are you a Communist?

Robeson replied that he was "violently anti-fascist."

Then the reporters asked if he followed the Communist party line.

"It depends on what you mean by the Communist Party line," he said. "Right now the Communist Party is against lynching. I'm against lynching."[4]

It was only a question by some reporters, but it signaled a serious change of mood in the United States. The word "communist" had become a danger signal for many people, and just having that word linked with one's name meant a person could be considered disloyal. There was nothing illegal about being a member of the Communist Party, but right-wing politicians were determined to make it look that way.

In less than a month, Robeson was called before a California group, the Joint Fact-Finding Committee on Un-American Activities in California, to answer questions about his activities. The committee was run by California State Senator Jack B. Tenney who subpoenaed teachers, government employees, and actors like Robeson to testify. Tenney later brought many bills into the California legislature, trying to stamp out what he thought was disloyal activity. Most of these bills never passed.

Robeson, of course, had only visited California occasionally. That didn't stop the committee from asking wide-ranging questions about places he had been and things he had done that had nothing to do with that state. The committee wanted to know about his trips to Russia and about the school that Paul, Jr., attended in the Soviet Union.

But the key question from Tenney was: "Are you a member of the Communist Party?"

"As far as I know," Robeson replied, "the Communist Party is a very legal one in the United States. I sort of characterize myself as an anti-Fascist and independent. If I wanted to join any party, I could just as conceivably join the Communist Party, more so today, than I could join the Republican or Democratic Party. But I am not a Communist."5

It was probably the strongest denial Robeson ever gave to the question of whether he was a Communist or not. In spite of that, some concert halls refused to rent space to Robeson after this. In Peoria, Illinois, the Shriner Mosque cancelled his contract and the mayor refused to let him use city hall. The school board of Albany, New York, also tried to keep him out of a junior high school auditorium, but Robeson won an injunction allowing his concert.

Robeson himself seemed to sense that a phase of his life was ending, that the stardom and crowd worship of so many years might fade away in the changing political mood. "It is irony," said his pianist Lawrence Brown, "that at the peak of his career and at the moment when I think he reached his zenith, he was more difficult to work with than during all the years before. He was in a terrible mood. He constantly felt he could not sing another concert."[6]

In March 1947, Robeson performed for 2,000 people at the University of Utah in Salt Lake City. A key part of the concert was his singing of "Joe Hill," a ballad written by Alfred Hayes and Earl Robinson about a radical union organizer. Hill had allegedly been framed for murder by Utah's copper companies some thirty years before and then executed by a firing squad. After the ballad, the audience sat silently for a moment, stunned that Robeson had the courage to sing the song in the heart of Utah. Then the auditorium rang with applause.

Just before the concert ended, Robeson walked out front to say: "You've heard my final concert for at least two years and perhaps for many more. I'm retiring here and now from concert work—I shall sing from now on, for my trade union and college friends; in other words, only at gatherings where I can sing what I please."[7]

Typical of the concerts Robeson gave after that was a trip to the Hawaiian Islands for twenty-seven performances sponsored by the International Longshoremen's and Warehousemen's Union. During this tour, the Honolulu newspapers devoted story after story to the question of whether Robeson was a Communist or not. One paper even listed eight groups which the House Un-American Activities Committee had called Communist front organizations and to which Robeson belonged.

The papers criticized Robeson's choice of songs as controversial and radical and claimed that he refused point-blank to deny he was a Communist. "The whole talk about Communism is absurd," Robeson told one paper. "Either we get along with the Communists, jump in the ocean or blow up the whole world. Saying you can't get along with Communists is like saying you can't get along with the birds."[8]

Early in 1948, an unusual political campaign took shape. A group of people who felt that Truman and the Democrats had abandoned the ideals of Franklin Roosevelt's New Deal decided to launch a new political party, the Progressive party. They persuaded former Vice President and Truman Cabinet–member Henry A. Wallace to run for president. Robeson served on the National Wallace for President Committee.

In April, representatives from across the country met in Chicago to organize the Progressive Party and write its political platform. Delegates represented trade unions and various nationalities and racial groups, but there were also Communist Party members present. Essie Robeson worked on the committee that drafted the platform along with lawyers, college professors, and business people. From the beginning the new party's attitude toward communism became a hot issue.

First one committee member proposed that the platform come out strongly against communism. Essie and others objected and eventually the motion was defeated. Then the committee proposed a plank condemning Soviet foreign policy as "territorial aggrandizement and power politics." Paul Robeson objected to it, and the final platform said that peace was the "joint responsibility of the Soviet Union and the United States."[9]

Finally, the convention moved on to speeches designed to inspire the crowd that would soon go out seeking votes.

Robeson, the magnificent stage performer, introduced Wallace to the crowd. At first the applauding audience shouted, "We want Wallace!" But soon they added: "Robeson for Vice President! We want Robeson!" Robeson walked off the stage, clearly embarrassed about the shouts from the crowd and anxious to make it clear that he did not want to run for office.

Over the next few months, Robeson went on tour to sing for Wallace, along with other entertainers like the folksinger Pete Seeger. Seeger had known Robeson since before World War II and continued to find him an impressive personality because of his "physique, voice, intonation, intellect and honesty." "In a truly democratic America," Seeger said, "Robeson would have been president."[10]

During the campaign, Robeson went to Washington to testify against the proposed Mundt-Nixon bill. This law would have required all Communist party members and Communist-allied groups to register with the federal government. Communists would be ineligible for passports or for federal jobs.

Robeson's testimony before a Senate committee quickly turned into an interrogation about his ideas on Russia and communism. Several times, senators asked him if he was a Communist. Finally he replied: "The question has become the very basis of the struggle for civil liberties. Nineteen men are about to go to jail for refusing to answer it. I am prepared to join them. I refuse to answer it."[11]

Protests against the bill continued, and finally the Senate dropped it. But the bill's defeat did not make touring for Wallace any easier. The House Un-American Activities Committee had stepped up its attacks on Wallace supporters. Many unions had deserted the campaign. Truman officials and even Truman himself accused Wallace of harboring Communists on his campaign staff.

In their swings through the South, Wallace and various

performers were the target for protesters throwing tomatoes and rotten eggs. Still Robeson carried on, and at times, he talked at street-corner meetings four and five times a day. Seeger wrote new songs making fun of the Democrats and Republicans, and Robeson sang his old favorites "Ol' Man River" and "Go Down, Moses."

In the end, the Progressives went the way that most third-party political movements have gone in the United States. Truman trounced Wallace, who received only 1,156,103 votes. Truman received 24 million votes and Thomas Dewey, the Republican candidate, received 22 million. Wallace's defeat seemed to encourage right-wing politicians. More than before, they felt that the public favored new attacks on the Communist party and its defenders. Their campaign against the left would devastate Robeson's career and personal life.

With teammates on the Rutgers University football squad.
Robeson twice made the All-American football team.

Champion debater Robeson with another member of the
Rutgers debating team. Robeson was also elected
to Phi Beta Kappa for his academic achievements.

Robeson in the musical Show Boat, *in which he gives his famous rendition of "Ol' Man River."*

Paul Robeson with his wife, Eslanda, in 1935.

**With son,
Paul Jr.,
in 1936.**

The great baritone at the piano.

*Robeson pickets the White House
to protest alleged employment
discrimination at the U.S. Bureau
of Engraving and Printing.*

Left to right: Former Vice President and 1948 presidential candidate Henry Wallace, physicist Albert Einstein, New Republic columnist Frank Kingdon, and Paul Robeson, in 1947.

Paul Robeson speaking at the World Congress of the Partisans of Peace in April 1949, at which he reportedly said that American blacks would never fight in a war against the Soviet Union. The speech marked a major turning point in Robeson's life.

Robeson sings at an open-air concert in Peekskill, New York. The concert provoked violent protests by demonstrators opposed to Robeson's views.

*Paul Robeson holds a press
conference to present evidence
of the lack of police protection
at the Peekskill concert.*

Robeson leaves Washington District Court in August, 1955, after a judge refused to order the State Department to reinstate his passport, which had been revoked five years earlier.

With Soviet premier
Nikita Khrushchev in 1958.

*Visiting a Moscow
machinery factory, 1958.*

*Robeson arrives at Kennedy airport in 1963
after five years abroad. Greeting him are
son, Paul, Jr., and daughter-in-law, Marilyn.*

"Unthinkable that American Negroes would go to war"

Suddenly, Robeson's concert career in the United States vanished practically overnight. Promoters would not hire him; auditoriums would not rent to him. Eighty-six out of eighty-six concerts planned for 1949 were cancelled. "I decided to go to Europe to resume my professional concerts for a very short period," Robeson said, "in order to make it perfectly clear that the world is wide and no few pressures could stop my career."[1]

The response that Robeson, Essie, and Lawrence Brown found in Europe was fantastic. In London, 8,000 seats at Albert Hall sold out for two Robeson concerts at five dollars a seat. In Manchester, 10,000 seats were put on sale in the morning and had sold out by noon.

The trip included many political events. In April 1949 Robeson traveled to the World Peace Congress in Paris. The event used as its symbol a dove of peace drawn by the artist Picasso and drew thousands of delegates from sixty countries in all. While he was there, a delegation of 2,000 students from colonial countries asked Robeson to address the conference about their desires for independence from their European masters. Robeson's speech became a major turning-point in his life and sparked vicious personal attacks on him that would continue for ten years.

One key statement he made touched a raw nerve in the United States: "It is unthinkable that American Negroes will go to war on behalf of those who have oppressed us for generations . . . against a country (the Soviet Union) which in one generation has raised our people to full human dignity of mankind," was how *The New York Times* quoted him.[2]

Reporters quickly sent stories about Robeson's speech to their papers in the United States, and some twisted his words so that it sounded as if he had flatly said that blacks would never fight the Soviet Union. His speech exploded like a grenade in a country already engulfed in heated hearings by the House Un-American Activities Committee. The nation was wrapped up in investigations of alleged former Communists and fights among public officials over whether the United States should press on to build the hydrogen bomb, an even bigger weapon than the atomic bomb it already had.

Suddenly, one of America's most prominent black men, Paul Robeson, had announced that millions of blacks were disenchanted with U.S. efforts to end racism and objected to the aggressive Cold War that their country was waging against the Russians. While Robeson sang his way across the Scandinavian countries, the storm bubbled and boiled. On every stop he was grilled again and again by reporters. Robeson stood by his words but noted that they were being taken out of context. His speech, he kept reminding the press, had focused on the struggle for peace, not on the need for war. But very few reporters seemed to pay attention.

Editorial writers in the United States denounced Robeson, including some in black newspapers. Walter White, the executive secretary of the National Association for the Advancement of Colored People, denied that Robeson spoke for blacks as a whole and said that black Americans would meet their responsibilities in wartime just like all other citizens. A top Connecticut official even went to the state police commissioner to demand that Robeson be kept out of the state and prevented from returning to his home in Enfield, but the request was denied. In the land of the free, it almost seemed that freedom of speech no longer existed.

Meanwhile, Robeson had reached Moscow, where he gave three concerts and also participated in a 150th birthday celebration for the black Russian poet Pushkin. After leaving Moscow, Robeson was apprehensive about his return to the United States. From the press reaction in Europe, he knew that he and Essie would arrive to find a hurricane. At La Guardia Airport in New York a horde of reporters and 20 policemen met his plane. As the couple pushed through the crowd, Robeson refused to answer questions and told the press that if they wanted to hear his opinions they should attend a giant welcome home rally planned for him in Harlem by the Council on African Affairs.

On June 19, 1949, the Sunday afternoon before the rally, the Robeson family had other more personal concerns. Pauli Robeson, by then a graduate of Cornell University with a degree in electrical engineering, planned to marry Marilyn Paula Greenberg, whom he had met in college. A quiet wedding was held in the Manhattan flat of a Congregational minister with just a few friends and relatives present. But somehow the press was tipped off. The fact that the ceremony involved Paul Robeson and that it was an interracial wedding turned the afternoon into a media circus. Dozens of reporters and photographers gathered outside the minister's home, along with several hundred white bystanders.

When wedding guests left the house, reporters mobbed Robeson. They followed the wedding party to a cab and started to shoot pictures of Pauli and Marilyn through the windows. Robeson could contain himself no longer and grabbed one of the cameras. "I have the greatest contempt for the democratic press," he told reporters. "Only something within me keeps me from smashing your cameras over your heads."3

That evening, Robeson was back among friends as 5,000 people gathered to hear him at the rally at Rockland Palace in Harlem. In a torrent, he poured out his frustrations about the lack of freedom for blacks in America, about the lynchings and poll taxes in the South. He outlined his struggles to help union members and Wallace and the Progressive party. He condemned the enslavement of colonial countries in Africa and Asia and said that the policies of the United States would only lead to big American companies taking control of nations like Nigeria, the Belgian Congo, Cuba, Guatemala, Vietnam, and Malaya. Again, Robeson defended the Soviet Union and said that millions of brown, yellow, and black people in that nation had been raised "to unbelievable industrial and social levels."

"Yes, I love this Soviet people more than any other nation," he said, "because of their suffering and sacrifices for us, the Negro people, the progressive people, the people of the future in this world."4 But he did not totally reject his native land. "I am born and bred in this America of ours. I want to love it. . . . But it's up to the rest of America when I shall love it with the same intensity that I love the Negro people from whom I spring."5

By now, it must have seemed to Robeson as if the United States government had declared war on him. As part of its hearings, the House Un-American Activities Committee summoned a parade of witnesses designed to embarrass Robeson and label him as a Communist party member and conspirator.

Among Robeson's chief accusers was Manning Johnson, a black who joined the Communist party during the 1930s and then quit in 1940. Johnson became a paid informer for the U.S. Justice Department and testified against union members, teachers, and political figures. At one point he admitted having lied in a hearing, but in spite of that the government kept him on the payroll and kept summoning him to testify.

That summer, Johnson told the subcommittee that Robeson was a Communist. After appearing in *The Emperor Jones,* Johnson said, Robeson had "developed a complex and delusions of grandeur, and set out to become a black Stalin among the Negroes of America."[6] Later Johnson was thoroughly discredited when he accused Dr. Ralph Bunche, a black American and United Nations official, of being a Communist party member. A loyalty board refuted Johnson's charges, and the Justice Department announced that it was investigating Johnson. But in the summer of 1949 his charges were accepted as flat truth and led to many newspaper stories that Robeson could do little to stop. When Robeson called news conferences to tell his story, he got little or no attention.

To further discredit Robeson the subcommittee would call several prominent blacks over the next couple of years to either denounce his opinions or to talk about his political activities. Many witnesses were under pressure from government officials to testify. Some were threatened with the loss of their jobs; some had been accused of being Communists themselves and felt that the only way out of their personal nightmare was to name names, including Paul Robeson's.

Jack "Jackie" Robinson, the first black to play in major league baseball, was asked to appear before the subcommittee to refute Robeson's statements about the Soviet Union. Robinson was stunned at being asked to denounce a man he had idolized while he was growing up. He didn't believe in everything that Robeson said, yet he felt that Robeson's stands against racism and discrimination were valid.

As Robinson thought about what to do, he was deluged by letters and phone calls from people on both sides of the issue. Yet he felt a sense of loyalty to Branch Rickey, the commissioner of baseball, who wanted him to testify. Finally, with pain and regret, he went before the committee to tell its members: "I've been asked to express my views on Paul Robeson's statement in Paris to the effect that American Negroes would refuse to fight in any war against Russia because we love Russia so much. I haven't any comment to make, except that the statement, if Mr. Robeson actually made it, sounds very silly to me. But he has a right to his personal views, and if he wants to sound silly when he expresses them in public, that's his business and not mine. He's still a famous ex-athlete and a great singer and actor."[7]

Later there would be other witnesses like Josh White, a black blues and folk singer. Years before, White had appeared with Robeson in the play, *John Henry*. He told the committee in 1950, "I have a great admiration for Mr. Robeson as an actor and great singer, and if what I read in the papers is true, I feel sad over the help he's been giving to people who despise America."[8]

Another black later caught in the attacks on Robeson was the actor Canada Lee, banned from television because he had belonged to left-wing groups labeled as Communist front organizations. Nearly penniless, he finally attacked Robeson and received a role in the film, *Cry, the Beloved Country*. But the struggle broke Lee; he died shortly after the movie was completed in 1952.

Ironically, all the troubles Robeson had had in the summer of 1949 had yet to reach their climax. One more explosive event would occur with major effects for him and the nation. Angry words were about to turn into physical violence.

"Like a rock unperturbed and unshaken"

In late August 1949, Paul Robeson was invited to sing at an open-air evening concert at the Lakeland Acres Picnic Grounds, a few miles from Peekskill, New York. Robeson had sung before at the site, a favorite summer vacation spot for garment workers from New York City.

The folk singer Pete Seeger was also to sing, and writer Howard Fast was going to be master of ceremonies for the event, sponsored by People's Artists, a folk-singing organization that booked artists to perform for labor unions and political groups. Like many other left-wing groups then, People's Artists was often under surveillance by the Federal Bureau of Investigation. Proceeds for the concert were to go to the Civil Rights Congress, a group organized in 1946 to work against racism and anti-Semitism. Robeson served as vice president for the congress.

Several days before the event, the local newspaper, the *Peekskill Evening Star,* launched an attack on the concert. People's Artists was called a red-front organization; Robeson was accused of having followers who were Communists. Then local groups such as the Peekskill Chamber of Commerce and Junior Chamber of Commerce joined the campaign. Veterans groups announced plans for a protest march during the concert. Of course, some in Peekskill supported the event and urged that New York officials send in the state police to prevent trouble. But the state did not respond.

The evening of the concert, August 27, turned out to be warm and beautiful. Hours before the starting time of 8:15, cars full of families expecting gentle music and picnic suppers under the stars poured into the area. In a bowl-shaped natural arena, a platform and 2,000 folding chairs were set up for the crowd.

But at about 7 P.M., hundreds of demonstrators also arrived, many wearing veterans' caps. The protesters quickly piled rocks in the entrance road to prevent any more concertgoers from driving in. Many protesters had been drinking heavily, and some carried clubs and brass knuckles. Clearly, they were looking for a reason to break loose and explode. Although a few police patrolled, the situation quickly became violent.

Robeson, warned in advance, never got to Peekskill. Pete Seeger also was stopped along the road before he reached the concert grounds and told that the concert had been canceled. But Howard Fast was trapped in the picnic grounds with the concertgoers. Nervously, Fast and a few dozen men organized fighting groups to keep the mob from reaching the women and children in the concert grounds. Time after time, they held off attackers armed with fence posts and knives. By then, the police had vanished.

As the protesters surged in clawing and punching, they shouted, "Lynch Robeson! Give us Robeson!" and "We're Hitler's boys! We'll finish his job!"[1] As a burning cross, a symbol of the Ku Klux Klan, blazed on a hillside, Fast and his fellow defenders locked arms and sang together: "We shall not—we shall not be moved!"

"They saw a line of Negroes and whites," Fast later wrote, "arms locked, ragged and bloody, standing calmly and singing—and the singing stopped them."[2] But not for long. First the attackers bombarded Fast and his men with rocks. Then they grabbed the chairs and books and pamphlets around the platform and set them on fire. Finally, at almost 10 o'clock, they left the scene. Although many calls had been made to the state police, troopers did not come until the violence ended, and no one was arrested. Several injured people had to be treated at a hospital.

Although some in Peekskill had joined the mob, many in that town and surrounding communities were outraged by the violence and what it said about their region. They held organizing meetings and set up the Westchester Committee for Law and Order, a group that invited Paul Robeson to sing at Peekskill again on a Sunday afternoon, September 4.

Three days after the concert, a giant rally of thousands of angry blacks also gathered in Harlem at the Golden Gate Ballroom. The huge crowd sweltered in the summer heat but sat for hours listening to speakers like Benjamin Davis, Howard Fast, and Paul Robeson. As Robeson walked in, Fast said, "He came in very proud and very troubled; and though I had seen him before in so many places in all the years our paths had crossed, I had never seen him like this."[3]

Robeson's friends in the unions whom he had supported for so many years in their strikes and organizing efforts pledged to defend any attacks on the second concert. But this support didn't mean that the battle had been won. The press continued to attack Robeson, and some editorial writers brushed off the Peekskill riot as an example of misguided patriotism by those opposed to Communism.

Throughout the town of Peekskill, some of the rioters who had protested the concert began hanging banners that read: "Wake Up America! Peekskill Did!"

The next problem for the concert organizers was to find a site to hold their event. The owner of Lakeland Acres, although sympathetic to the cause, was afraid of new violence. Other property owners also refused. Finally, a refugee from Nazi Germany offered a site which had once been a country club but now was an open area of meadows. There could be no chairs, so concertgoers would have to picnic on the grass.

The day of the concert, it was clear that the organizers were well prepared. Leon Straus of the International Fur and Leather Workers Union organized a command post of several thousand workers who came to set up the grounds and provide security. Cars and buses poured into the concert grounds and parked in orderly rows until some 25,000 people had arrived. The opponents of the concert had predicted that they would organize 30,000 marchers for another protest, but in the end, they only mustered about 1,000.

In preparation for possible attacks, the union members formed a border guard of 2,500 men, lined up shoulder to shoulder between the concertgoers and the protesters on the fringe of the concert grounds. Also on hand were 1,000 state and local police. But soon police clashed with union guards. The police wanted the union members to pull back in, closer to the concertgoers, but the union members refused. They wanted to maintain a safety zone around the picnickers. To retaliate, the police pulled out.

Then the protesting veterans began to throw rocks at the guards. Under the hail of missiles, the guards remained at their posts, holding the shouting, cursing protesters at bay. "You'll get in," the veterans taunted them, "but you won't get out."[4]

The police also set up a barricade on the road to keep any other concertgoers from arriving. Several more cars did come down the road and tried to get through. Some black concertgoers were dragged out of the cars by the veterans and beaten.

Robeson arrived at about noon and on the advice of

security people he stayed in his car until the concert was about to start. Although the crowd and the union organizers were confident and cheerful, believing that a great moral victory had been won, Robeson was worried. He sensed that more violence was still possible that day.

In the meantime, the concert organizers decided to move the sound truck behind the area where Robeson would sing so that no snipers would try to shoot at him from up in the hills above. Fifteen workers also stood behind him and at his sides as he sang. It was a human wall of protectors to shield him from danger. "They were white workers and Negro workers," Fast said, "and this giant of a man was one of the very, very few intellectuals in the whole land who had not fled from their side, who had not betrayed them, who had not crawled for cover, but stood like a rock unperturbed and unshaken."[5]

Soon the songs began and music by Handel and Bach floated over the crowd. Robeson won a standing ovation for "Ol' Man River." Seeger sang a number he composed only a few months before—"If I Had a Hammer"—destined to become an American classic. The only reminder of the angry forces on the fringes of the concert was a police helicopter that buzzed over the stage.

But by 4 P.M., when the crowd climbed into cars for the ride home, the day turned ugly. On each of the three exit roads out of the concert grounds, the mob raged. Protesters heaved rocks at the cars, breaking windshields and denting fenders, in some cases in front of policemen who laughed at the concertgoers. Drivers and passengers were covered with slivers of glass.

As Robeson's car passed by, police with clubs flogged at the car and smashed the windshield. He was not injured, but many others were. "Never in all my life have I seen so much blood; never have I seen so many people so cruelly cut and bleeding so badly," said Howard Fast.[6] All over Westchester the hospitals were crowded with people who had suffered cuts and bruises in the attacks. At the very end, police had surged onto the concert grounds and arrested twenty-five union member–guards.

When it was all settled and the news went out to the rest of the world, there was a strong outcry against Peekskill, and the American Civil Liberties Union launched an investigation. The ACLU concluded that police deliberately withheld protection from the first concert. State troopers had tried to preserve law and order at the second concert, but county police fraternized with the rioters, the ACLU said.

Newspaper after newspaper, many of which had condemned some of Robeson's past speeches, harshly criticized the rioters. "True Americans must feel deep shame and concern for the quality of citizenship that believes it is defending its country by catcalls and boos and rocks thrown at passing automobiles," said the *New York Herald Tribune*.[7]

"Veterans' organizations in Westchester County, New York, lowered themselves to the level of the Ku Klux Klan," said the *St. Louis Post-Dispatch*.[8]

Yet many believe that the Peekskill concerts marked a turning point in American history. It was as if the violence of the right-wing mob provided American officials with the stamp of approval for what would happen in the next few years. Many suspect that the political witchhunts of suspected Communists, the demands for loyalty oaths, the sedition trials would never have taken place if Peekskill had not happened first.

"My people died to build this country"

By 1949, a nationwide campaign was steaming along against anyone linked to the Communist party or to left-wing groups. Thousands, besides Robeson, suffered in the government investigations, trials, and hearings. Some went to jail; others lost their jobs because of publicity about their political views. Fear and harassment even drove a few to suicide. In 1953, a New York couple active in Communist causes, Julius and Ethel Rosenberg, were executed in the electric chair for espionage. They denied being spies, and the question of their guilt is still debated decades later.

In many ways the attacks on Robeson were typical of the national hysteria. But they had a unique side. Robeson's political enemies resolved to make him disappear, to make it seem as if he had never existed. Here was a man who had had great impact on the concert stage, on political thought among blacks, even in the sports world. Now right-wing forces fought to erode his power and rob Robeson of his voice and his chance to answer his accusers.

Shortly after Peekskill, Robeson was called as a defense witness in the New York trial of eleven Communist party workers accused of working to overthrow the government of the United States. Among the defendants was his longtime friend, Benjamin Davis. Robeson wanted to tell the court that he had never heard Davis or the other defendants plot against the government. But the judge refused to let him testify and told Robeson: "I can't find from anything in these questions that you have any knowledge of the facts that are relevant in this case."[1]

Robeson said later that he had lost faith in the courts. He no longer believed that judges in the United States wanted to hear the truth. After that, Robeson returned to singing and speaking in a tour arranged by the Council on African Affairs. But again the owners of halls in city after city canceled contracts and veterans groups picketed his performances.

In Detroit, the fire marshal insisted that the type of chairs in a meeting hall where Robeson was to sing were illegal. Before the concert could go on, 8,000 chairs had to be wired together. Some city councils passed resolutions urging people not to attend the concerts. Newspapers wrote editorials condemning Robeson. In spite of these attacks, thousands still packed Robeson's concerts when he could arrange them.

The pressure didn't silence Robeson. At a banquet in New York in November 1949, he told the crowd that the only real patriots in the United States were those who sought friendship with the Soviet Union, which he said had fought discrimination and set an example for the rest of the world. In June 1950, Robeson helped organize a Chicago conference that aimed to fight racism in labor unions. That same month, he denounced the United States intervention in the Korean War on the side of South Korea during a rally in New York.

Many of his speeches directly challenged his accusers. He told one audience that Communists "represent a new way of life in the world, a new way that has won the allegiance of almost half the world's population. . . . They need no apologies."[2]

Soon, it became impossible to find a recording of "Ol' Man River" or any Robeson record in any music shop, and record companies refused to let Robeson make new albums. Robeson responded by producing two albums under his own label, Othello Recording Corporation, and marketed his records by mail.

In November 1950, he also helped launch a monthly journal, *Freedom*, that was published for almost five years out of offices in Harlem. It carried a regular column by Robeson titled, "Here's My Story," but also ran articles by W. E. B. Du Bois, Lorraine Hansberry, and others and served as a strong voice for black activism during a time when it was difficult to speak out about injustice.

Meanwhile, the campaign to make Robeson disappear marched on. Books written on music and black leaders omitted his name; newspapers refused to cover his press conferences or to print his replies to charges against him. Rutgers University alumni wrote to the school demanding that Robeson's name be struck from the rolls of graduates and that the school revoke his degree. They never succeeded, but one sports annual deleted Robeson's name from a list of football All-Americans.

FBI agents tapped Robeson's phone and read his mail. The Robeson family even claimed that informants monitored doctors' reports on his health. Soon Robeson, once one of the highest-paid concert artists in the nation, saw his income shrink to next to nothing. It sank from more than $100,000 in the 1940s to an estimated $6,000 in 1952. The Robesons were forced to sell the estate in Connecticut that Essie had loved so much. Robeson's eyes naturally turned toward Europe where he could still rent halls easily. He soon arranged speaking engagements in several foreign countries.

But on July 28, 1950, U.S. State Department agents demanded that Robeson turn in his passport. On his attorney's advice, he refused to do so but the government canceled the passport and ordered border officials to stop him from leaving the country. The State Department said his travel abroad conflicted with the best interests of the United States. Passports for Essie and Paul, Jr., were also cancelled.

When Robeson demanded to see Secretary of State Dean Acheson, State Department officials offered to return his passport if he would sign a pledge not to make any speeches in foreign countries. But Robeson refused, and from then on, his only recourse seemed to be the courts. In December, he sued to try to get his passport back. It launched a long court battle lasting many years as judge after judge rejected his case. Over the next few years, he would file many applications for passports, only to be rejected time after time. At one point, he was asked to sign a statement swearing he was not a Communist, but he refused. "Under no conditions would I think of signing any such affidavit . . . it is a complete contradiction of the rights of American citizens," Robeson said.[3]

Meanwhile, invitations poured in from other countries, none of which Robeson could accept. In January 1952, he was asked to speak at a mine workers meeting in Vancouver, British Columbia. Robeson had no passport, but generally Americans did not need passports to get into Canada. At the Canadian border officials were waiting for him. He was told that if he tried to leave the United States, he could be sent to jail for five years and be fined $10,000. For several hours, union officials and Robeson argued with U.S. officials. But Robeson had to settle for singing for the union group via long-distance phone from Seattle.

A few months later, the miners and Robeson achieved a victory at the Canadian-American border in the Vancouver area. There 40,000 Canadian and American citizens stood on both sides of the border at the Peace Arch Park as Robeson gave an outdoor concert. For forty-five minutes he sang, accompanied by Lawrence Brown. Traffic was blocked for miles around and the border had to be closed because of the congestion.

Despite the obstacles thrown up against him, Robeson made several concert tours in the early 1950s. During a "birthday" tour from April 6 to June 2, 1952, for example, he raised $50,000 to aid the National Negro Labor Council, the Council on African Affairs and *Freedom.*

Many times, he was limited to performing in churches where ministers and congregations bravely ignored the attacks on him. Even that was sometimes impossible. In 1952, Robeson was scheduled to sing at a black church in Chicago. At first the FBI pressured the minister and congregation to stop the concert but got nowhere. Then, the mortgage holders who held a $100,000 loan on the church threatened to foreclose if the concert went on. So the church had to cancel out. Fifteen thousand, both black and white, later turned out in Washington Park to hear Robeson.

Although the Robesons bravely continued speaking out for those fighting for independence in colonial nations, against discrimination in the United States and against the Korean War, the strain of the struggle aged both Paul and Essie during the early 1950s. Photos show their faces growing lined with care and worry, their hair turning gray quickly. Even Essie was summoned before the Senate Investigating Committee headed by Senator Joseph McCarthy to answer questions about Communism.

A particularly sharp blow for the Robesons came in the mid 1950s when the Council on African Affairs was forced to close down. After the U.S. attorney general had labeled the group as a subversive organization, it had lost membership and contributions and could no longer stay afloat financially.

Some friends still supported Robeson. Citizens abroad were particularly puzzled about the attacks on him. British theater people invited Robeson to return to London for another production of *Othello*. Miners who had met Robeson during the production of *Proud Valley* invited him to a festival in Wales. Trade union members and other citizens in England petitioned President Eisenhower asking him to give back Robeson's passport.

The National Church of Nigeria named Robeson "Champion of African Freedom," an award granted for his service to Africa. In the United States, college students began opening their arms to him. Among those asking him to perform: the University of Chicago, Swarthmore College, and Northwestern, Kansas State, and Wisconsin universities.

Some support for Robeson, however, caused new problems. The Soviet Union remained staunchly behind him and in 1949 even named a mountain after him. Then in 1953, Robeson won Russia's Stalin Peace Prize, which carried a $25,000 cash award. Robeson reacted warmly. The prize, he said, will "spur me on to greater efforts than ever before to serve the cause of peace and to aid in building a triumphant peace movement in the United States."4

But Robeson had to fight for years to keep from having to pay taxes on the money. Normally, winners of such foreign prizes, such as the Nobel awards, were exempt from taxes. But in Robeson's case, the Internal Revenue Service argued that the Soviets were paying him for past services.

Frequently, blacks were summoned to appear before the House Un-American Activities Committee to denounce Robeson or to repudiate his ideas in writing. The idea seemed to be to isolate Robeson from his own people; to make him look as if he had no support among blacks. Yet Robeson remained gracious throughout this trying period when pressure was being put on many black artists. Singer Harry Belafonte, for example, was told at one point during the 1950s that he could not get a film role unless he signed a statement saying that he had campaigned for Henry Wallace because he was paid for it. When Belafonte asked Robeson if he found that objectionable, Robeson told him, "No, there are few enough jobs for blacks as it is, and I wouldn't tell a black what to do."[5]

For years, as witnesses attacked Robeson in Congress and insinuated that he was part of a Communist conspiracy, Robeson was denied the chance to face his accusers. Then in July 1956, Robeson was called before the House Un-American Activities Committee during an investigation of so-called "unauthorized use" of U.S. passports.

Robeson and his attorney appeared at 10 A.M. that day in a caucus room of the Old House Office Building in Washington, D.C. As the meeting began, the committee chairman stated that at other hearings it had been revealed that Communists had often gotten American passports on the pretext that they were traveling for business or pleasure. Once overseas, he said, they attended Communist-backed conferences and aided propaganda efforts in Communist countries. The question was, he said, should the government refuse passports to those going to such conferences?

Repeatedly, the committee members pressed Robeson to say whether he was a member of the Communist party as other witnesses and informers had alleged.

"What do you mean by the Communist Party?" Robeson retorted. As far as I know it is a legal party like the Republican Party and the Democratic Party. Do you mean which, belonging to a party of Communists or belonging to a party of people who have sacrificed for my people and for all Americans and workers, that they can live in dignity?"[6]

When pressed further, Robeson invoked the Fifth Amendment to the Constitution as hundreds of witnesses had done during the Red Scare of the 1950s. The purpose of the Fifth Amendment is to protect a witness against self-incrimination, against having to testify against one self. But in many cases, these witnesses invoked it not to avoid discussing their own membership in the Communist party or left-wing groups but so that they would not have to accuse others of being Communists.

What complicated the situation was that belonging to the Communist party by itself was not illegal. Because of that, many times the committee tried to force witnesses to answer. In this hearing, Richard Arens, director of the subcommittee, asked Robeson if he honestly thought that if he answered the question about Communism he would disclose information that could be used against him in a criminal trial.

Robeson replied, "The Fifth Amendment has nothing to do with criminality. The Chief Justice of the Supreme Court, (Earl) Warren, has been very clear on that in many speeches that the Fifth Amendment does not have anything to do with the inference of criminality."[7]

Next, committee members questioned Robeson again and again about his friends and about past testimony of paid informers who had called him a Communist. Once more, he refused to answer. Committee member Gordon Scherer asked Robeson about his trips to Russia and statements he'd made defending Russia.

Robeson: "I would say in Russia I felt for the first time like a full human being, and no colored prejudice like in Mississippi and no colored prejudice like in Washington and it was the first time I felt like a human being, where I did not feel the pressure of colored as I feel in this committee today."

Scherer: "Why do you not stay in Russia?"

Robeson: "Because my father was a slave, and my people died to build this country, and I am going to stay here and have a part of it just like you. And no Fascist-minded people will drive me from it. Is that clear?"[8]

Robeson was also grilled about his views on Stalin and on slave labor camps in Russia. "As far as I know about the slave camps," he said, "they were Fascist prisoners who had murdered millions of the Jewish people and who would have wiped out millions of the Negro people could they have gotten a hold of them."[9]

It sounded as if Robeson still gave his unqualified support to the Russians, but another statement hinted that he was well aware of Soviet problems: "I will discuss Stalin when I may be among the Russian people some day singing for them, and I will discuss it there. It is their problem."[10]

At the hearing, Robeson begged to read an explanation of his views, but the committee wouldn't even let him enter it into the record, much less read it. So he gave a statement to the press. He had not been part of any conspiracy, he said. It should be plain to anyone that if the government had evidence against him, they would have put him in jail.

Many have asked about Robeson, as they have about others, if they were not Communists, why didn't they say so. Robeson told the press: "In 1946 at a hearing in California, I testified under oath that I was not a member of the Communist Party. Since then, I have refused to give testimony to that fact. There is no mystery in this. I have made it a matter of principle to refuse to comply with any demand that infringes upon the constitutional rights of all Americans."[11]

He was not a Communist, said his son, Paul Robeson, Jr. "But if he had said he wasn't, then he couldn't have used the Fifth Amendment, and they could have asked him if his sister, brother or friends were Communists."[12]

"The American people are growing up"

But Robeson's confrontation with the House Un-American Activities Committee proved to be the last gasp of his attackers.

In the late 1950s, the entertainment world and the public were tiring of the crusade against so-called Communists. Merely knowing someone who was under attack or contributing money to the "wrong" organization or subscribing to a left-wing publication no longer seemed like "crimes."

In 1954, the Senate censured Senator Joseph McCarthy, chief persecutor of those suspected to be Communists. The death of Joseph Stalin in 1953 and the end of the Korean War in 1955 had also softened America's hard stand against the Russians.

Many Americans began to accept Robeson's political activism and to listen to what he had to say. The concert halls that had once shut him out began to open up again. In the summer of 1957 Robeson appeared five times in California and sang to 10,000 people in all. If he hadn't been returning to New York, he could have done another fifteen concerts in the Bay Area alone because there was such demand to hear him.

Robeson had not changed his message. He continued to speak out strongly against segregation and in support of friendship with the Soviet Union and China. The difference was, Robeson said, "the American people are growing up."[1]

The fact that Robeson had been a political outcast for almost ten years was becoming an embarrassment to the nation. Across the world, many nations were aware that Robeson was about to celebrate his sixtieth birthday. In India, the future prime minister, Indira Gandhi, organized a national committee to sponsor a Paul Robeson birthday party in India. In Moscow, East Berlin, Peking, and many African nations, there were parties as well for Robeson's April 9 birthday.

Then in May 1958, America's new acceptance of Robeson peaked as he gave a sold-out concert on that star-studded concert stage, Carnegie Hall in New York City. When word got out that he would appear there for the first time in almost a dozen years, every seat was sold two weeks in advance. It turned out to be more than a mere concert because Robeson poured out his soul to the crowd that night. A major battle had been won, a turning point had come in his life.

His choice of music spanned the world: Negro spirituals like "Every Time I Feel the Spirit" and "Didn't My Lord Deliver Daniel"; the "Chinese Children's Song"; "Christ Lag in Todesbanden" by Bach. Although at first his voice seemed tense, as the concert went on, he warmed up and sang superbly. He held the audience completely in his hands during his songs and the speeches in between. Then he began "We Are Climbing Jacob's Ladder" and invited the audience to join in. The emotion in the crowd bubbled to the surface as everyone seemed to join the fight that Robeson sang about. At the conclusion, the packed house stood to roar its approval.

After a second similar concert at Carnegie Hall, Robeson announced that he had won his battle to get his passport back and would soon leave the country.

What happened was that the Supreme Court had ruled in favor of three citizens who had lost their passports and said that Congress had not authorized the State Department to cancel anyone's passport because of beliefs or associations. In response, State issued passports to the plaintiffs in those lawsuits and also to Robeson.

Soon Robeson received many offers to appear in concerts in the United States and abroad, and by July he had gone to Europe. Soon he was touring Russia. He visited Yalta in Russia's Crimea and was welcomed by Premier Nikita Khrushchev. Toward the end of the year, he returned to London to sing in St. Paul's Cathedral to a crowd of 4,000 people inside the cathedral and 5,000 standing outside.

That fall, Robeson published a book, *Here I Stand*, that was part autobiography, part essay touching on his opinions. No major American publisher would touch the book, and when it came out, most major newspapers refused to review it, although Robeson was no longer the political outcast he had been for so long.

The book's editor, Lloyd L. Brown, wrote to *The New York Times* to ask why there had been no review, and an editor replied that the paper could find no record about *Here I Stand*. "I just want to assure you that we carefully consider every book we receive and I am certain that any book by Paul Robeson would not have been rejected for review if in the judgment of the editors it merited attention,"[2] the editor said.

Although Robeson had won a major victory with the return of his passport, his health was shattered. Early in January 1959, he became ill and had to be hospitalized in Moscow while on a visit to Russia. Over the next four years, he was in and out of the hospital, to treat a circulatory disease and mental problems.

He was released from the hospital so that he could appear in a new production of *Othello* in Stratford-on-Avon in England, although the doctors strictly limited how much he could work each week. But this time, his *Othello* did not win the acclaim of his earlier productions. His voice was going; his acting career appeared to be over.

In 1960, Essie visited with the folksinger Pete Seeger and his wife, Toshi, in London and told them that Paul had made himself ill by trying to take on all the world's problems. "Paul must realize that no one person can do everything," she warned.3

Nevertheless, Robeson kept up his speeches and public appearances, shuttling back and forth between Moscow and Western Europe. He made a concert tour in the British Isles and in 1960 he performed in Australia and New Zealand.

But then in early 1961, suffering from mental depression, Robeson re-entered a hospital in Moscow, and for the next few months a wave of newspaper stories and rumors claimed that Robeson had become disillusioned with communism and the socialist countries. Pauli Robeson and Essie denied the reports, but the rumors persisted for several years.

Was there any basis to them? Robert Robinson, the black American who spent forty-four years inside the Soviet Union, tells what the rumors were inside that country. According to Robinson, Robeson gave a concert for workers at the factory where Robinson was working in 1961. In spite of his failing health, Robeson still captivated the workers with his music.

But one of his songs shocked Robinson. It was a Yiddish song about the sufferings of the Jews that seemed to beg for the persecution to stop. Robinson wondered "whether Robeson, who was so determined to see only good in the Soviet system, was even aware of Soviet anti-Semitism. I decided that he must be, and that perhaps he knew what he was doing."4

Robinson claimed he later heard from Communist

party members of a painful meeting between Soviet Premier Nikita Khrushchev and Robeson. The report was that Robeson was invited to Khrushchev's villa and while there had asked the premier about the rumors about Soviet anti-Semitism. Khrushchev angrily told Robeson not to meddle in Russian politics. Soon after, Robeson left Russia for East Germany.

Robinson claimed that following this incident he never heard Robeson's records played on the radio in Russia again. "Robeson was the darling of the Soviets as long as he blindly toed their ideological line, but was made a non-person when he questioned Soviet domestic policies," Robinson said.[5]

Howard Fast, a longtime friend and a fighter with Robeson for many liberal causes, doubts that he ever changed his mind about the Soviet Union. "I don't think Paul ever had regrets about his closeness to the Soviet Union," Fast said. "The Russians adored him. He was a national hero in the Soviet Union to a point where any meeting, any place where he sang was overwhelmed with audiences. Here, he was persecuted and hounded, so you can see he had no reason ever to change his feelings about the Soviet Union."[6]

Paul Robeson, Jr., also called Robinson's story "utter nonsense from beginning to end. Khrushchev and my father were friends. The story may have been a rumor floated by Stalinists in Russia, the same people who overthrew Khrushchev a few years later."[7]

At any rate, in December 1963, Paul and Essie Robeson flew home to New York. As reporters hovered nearby, a thin and gray-haired Robeson, sixty-five years old, hugged Pauli and Marilyn and their two teen-age children, David and Susan. Essie fielded questions from reporters and insisted that Robeson was not coming home because he was upset with Communism but because it was Christmas.

After a short stay with their son, the Robesons took a house in Harlem and lived quietly behind tightly closed doors. Their phone was unlisted; they frequently did not answer their mail. Very few people visited their home. But Robeson did make some public appearances over the next few years and also wrote articles when public events called for it. He spoke at the funeral of his friend, Benjamin J. Davis.

In the spring of 1965, he appeared at a "Salute to Paul Robeson," sponsored by the Negro freedom magazine, *Freedomways,* where Ossie Davis, the actor and playwright, served as master of ceremonies. He made a long speech that evening, talking about his joy at seeing new opportunities for blacks in music and the theater. After visiting many socialist countries, Robeson said, he had also decided that the various systems of government should compete among themselves peacefully "and the people can decide for themselves" which is best.[8]

The Negro people's march toward freedom is necessary and inevitable, he said. "Most important is the recognition that achieving these demands in no way lessens the democratic rights of white American citizens. On the contrary, it will enormously strengthen the base of democracy for all Americans."[9]

Soon, Robeson's poor health ended his public appearances. In December, Essie, a fellow worker for human rights and peace, fell ill and died on the eve of her sixty-ninth birthday. She had had cancer for several years but had kept it a secret from all but her family and closest friends. Not only had she been a strong supporter for Robeson, but she had also helped shape his thought and his career.

Paul Robeson remained for a time in Harlem, but later moved in with his sister in Philadelphia. Although he lived on for seven years after Essie's death, he rarely appeared outside his home, and was himself hospitalized several times.

In spite of his quiet life, his name and reputation grew as Americans tried to make up for the damage done to him in the 1950s. Magazines ran profiles of him, and *Ebony* magazine named him one of the "ten most important black men in American history." Rutgers hung his photograph again in a gallery of football players in the college gym and named a new student center after him. Actors Equity set up an award in his name and named him the first winner. He was given a doctor of law degree by Lincoln University in Pennsylvania, his father's alma mater.

In April 1973, to celebrate Robeson's seventy-fifth birthday, parties were held worldwide, including one at Carnegie Hall, put on by Harry Belafonte and other friends. Robeson could not attend, but he sent a tape recording giving his thanks. He told the crowd he was the "same" Paul that had fought lifelong for freedom, peace, and brotherhood. His heart was with blacks and other minority groups still seeking freedom, he said. In his usual forthright way he saluted those in Africa, Latin America, and Asia who sought independence from colonial governments, and he referred to the Vietnamese who he said "have once again turned back an imperialist aggressor" in the Vietnam War.[10]

Then in December 1975, he was admitted to Presbyterian Medical Center in Philadelphia after a mild stroke. His condition grew worse until on January 23, 1976, he died at age of seventy-seven. Thousands paid their respects to Robeson in the Harlem funeral home where his body lay. Four days later, more than 5,000 people attended his funeral service at the Mother African Methodist Episcopal Church in Harlem.

His granddaughter, Susan Robeson, twenty-two when he died, was overwhelmed by the crowds. "I had never experienced such an outpouring of love and dedication for one human being, and it made me feel proud and strong," she later wrote.[11]

America, perhaps belatedly, had found one of its heroes again.

Epilogue

In death, as in life, Paul Robeson continues to inspire controversy, and no doubt, arguments about what his life meant will go on for decades. His family and friends have jealously protected his memory and have rightfully tried to correct many of the wrongs done to him in his lifetime.

Typical is the controversy that arose when actor James Earl Jones appeared in Washington, D.C., and on Broadway in a one-man play about Robeson, shortly after Robeson's death. More than fifty black artists and political leaders took out a two-page advertisement in a Broadway publication to condemn the play. They charged that the drama, by a black playwright, distorted many facts in Robeson's life and failed to show him as the revolutionary hero that he really was.

At the same time, students of civil rights have become more convinced than ever of how forward-looking Paul Robeson really was and what a strong influence he was on black leaders to come.

Long before such causes became popular crusades, he spoke out against apartheid and colonial domination of third world nations. He stood for truth, justice, and freedom not just in his own country but worldwide and not just for blacks but for all oppressed people.

Notes

Chapter One

1. Paul Robeson, "Address at Welcome Home Rally," in *Paul Robeson Speaks*, ed. Philip S. Foner (New York: Brunner/ Mazel Inc., 1978), 201.
2. Paul Robeson, *Here I Stand* (1958; reprint, Boston: Beacon Press, 1971), 10.
3. Ibid., 9.
4. Eslanda Goode Robeson, *Paul Robeson, Negro* (New York: Harper & Brothers, 1930), 16.
5. Ibid., 9.
6. Paul Robeson, *Here I Stand*, 20.
7. Eslanda Robeson, *Paul Robeson, Negro*, 20.
8. Paul Robeson, *Here I Stand*, 15.
9. Ibid., 16.
10. Ibid., 12.
11. Ibid., 17.

Chapter Two

1. Booker T. Washington, "The Atlanta Exposition Address," in *The Negro Since Emancipation*, ed. Harvey Wish (New Jersey: Prentice-Hall Inc., 1964), 46.
2. William E. B. Du Bois, "The Talented Tenth," in *The Negro Since Emancipation*, 73.

3. Paul Robeson, "The Legacy of W. E. B. Du Bois," *Freedom-ways*, Winter 1965, 36.
4. Paul Robeson, *Here I Stand*, 19.
5. Ibid., 20.
6. Ibid., 21.
7. Paul Robeson, "Address at Welcome Home Rally," reprinted in *Paul Robeson Speaks*, 202.
8. Paul Robeson, *Here I Stand*, 22.
9. Ibid., 112.
10. Ibid., 25.
11. Interview with Robert Van Gelder, *The New York Times*, 14 January 1944.
12. Ibid.
13. Paul Robeson, "The New Idealism: Oration at Rutgers Graduation," 10 June 1919, in *Paul Robeson Speaks*, 64.

Chapter Three

1. Ron Thomas, "NFL's Only Black Coach," *San Francisco Chronicle*, 27 January 1988, Sports section.
2. Eslanda Robeson, *Paul Robeson, Negro*, 72.
3. Pearl S. Buck with Eslanda Goode Robeson, *American Argument* (New York: John Day Co., 1949), 25.
4. Ibid., 26.
5. "An Actor's Wanderings and Hopes," *The Messenger*, October 1924, reprinted in *Paul Robeson Speaks*, 68.
6. Marie Seton, *Paul Robeson* (London: Dennis Dobson, 1958), 12.

Chapter Four

1. Eslanda Robeson, *Paul Robeson, Negro*, 73.
2. Ibid., 75.
3. Louis Sheaffer, *O'Neill: Son and Artist* (Boston: Little Brown & Co., 1973), 37.
4. Ibid., 142.
5. Ibid., 135.
6. Ibid., 138.
7. Ibid.
8. Ibid., 140.

9. Ibid., 139.
10. Paul Robeson, "Reflections on O'Neill's Plays," *Opportunity*, December 1924, reprinted in *Paul Robeson Speaks*, 70.
11. Sheaffer, *O'Neill: Son and Artist*, 141.
12. Arthur and Barbara Gelb, *O'Neill* (New York: Harper & Brothers, 1962), 555.
13. Sheaffer, *O'Neill: Son and Artist*, 143.
14. Dorothy Butler Gilliam, *Paul Robeson: All-American* (Washington, D.C.: The New Republic Book Co., 1976), 38.
15. Seton, *Paul Robeson*, 37.

Chapter Five

1. Buck, *American Argument*, 40.
2. Paul Robeson, *Here I Stand*, 32.
3. Emma Goldman, *Living My Life* (1931; reprint, New York: Dover, 1970), 980.
4. Seton, *Paul Robeson*, 40.
5. Max Eastman, *Love and Revolution* (New York: Random House, 1964), 468–469.
6. Susan Robeson, *The Whole World in His Hands* (New Jersey: Citadel Press, 1981), 101.
7. Buck, *American Argument*, 12.
8. Eslanda Robeson, *Paul Robeson, Negro*, 124.
9. Interview in *The New York Times*, 5 April 1931, quoted in *Paul Robeson, Negro*, 81.
10. Ibid., 82.
11. Buck, *American Argument*, 154–55.
12. Eslanda Robeson, *Paul Robeson, Negro*, 127–28.
13. Ibid., 133.
14. Ibid., 137.

Chapter Six

1. Paul Robeson, *Here I Stand*, 31.
2. As quoted in Anatol I. Schlosser, *Paul Robeson: His Career in the Theatre, in Motion Pictures, and on the Concert Stage* (Ph.D. diss., New York University, 1970), 101.

3. Cedric Hardwicke as told to James Brough, *A Victorian in Orbit* (London: Methuen & Co., 1961), 129.
4. Alexander Woollcott, *While Rome Burns,* (New York: Viking Press, 1934), 125.
5. Ibid., 126.

Chapter Seven

1. Seton, *Paul Robeson*, 47.
2. Paul Robeson, *Here I Stand*, 33.
3. Buck, *An American Argument*, 40.
4. Ibid., 41.
5. Schlosser, *Paul Robeson: His Career*, 110.
6. Ibid., 111.
7. Seton, *Paul Robeson*, 55.
8. Schlosser, *Paul Robeson: His Career*, 119.
9. Seton, *Paul Robeson*, 54.
10. As quoted in Eslanda Robeson, *Paul Robeson, Negro*, 156.
11. Marvin Rosenberg, *The Masks of Othello* (Berkeley: University of California Press, 1961), 152.
12. Margaret Webster, *Don't Put Your Daughter on the Stage* (New York: Knopf, 1972), 106.

Chapter Eight

1. Eslanda Robeson, *Paul Robeson, Negro*, 143.
2. Interview with Paul Robeson, Jr.
3. Interview, *New York World Telegram*, 30 August 1933, reprinted in *Paul Robeson Speaks*, 85.
4. "Wife Sues Robeson," *The New York Times*, 26 June 1932.
5. Interview with Paul Robeson, Jr.
6. Edward Mapp, *Blacks in Films* (Metuchen, New Jersey: Scarecrow Press, 1972), 24.

Chapter Nine

1. Interview by Vern Smith, *Daily Worker*, 15 January 1935, reprinted in *Paul Robeson Speaks*, 94.

2. Seton, *Paul Robeson*, 84.
3. Robert Robinson with Jonathan Slevin, *Black on Red: My 44 Years Inside the Soviet Union* (Washington, D.C.: Acropolis Books Ltd., 1988), 312.
4. Interview by Vern Smith, reprinted in *Paul Robeson Speaks*, 95.
5. Interview by Benjamin Davis, *Sunday Worker*, 10 May 1936, reprinted in *Paul Robeson Speaks*, 106.
6. Ibid., 107.
7. Interview by Julia Dorn, *New Theatre*, July 1935, reprinted in *Paul Robeson Speaks*, 101.
8. Interview with Paul Robeson, Jr.
9. Interview, *Irish Workers' Voice*, 23 February 1935, reprinted in *Paul Robeson Speaks*, 485.
10. Robinson, *Black on Red*, 15.
11. Interview by Benjamin Davis, reprinted in *Paul Robeson Speaks*, 108.

Chapter Ten

1. Anatol I. Schlosser, "Paul Robeson in Film: An Iconoclast's Quest for a Role," in "Paul Robeson, the Great Forerunner," special edition of *Freedomways* (New York: International Publishing Co., 1985), 77.
2. Interview by Benjamin Davis, reprinted in *Paul Robeson Speaks*, 107.
3. Eslanda Goode Robeson, *African Journey* (New York: John Day Co., 1945), 17.
4. Ibid., 19.
5. Ibid.
6. As quoted in Susan Robeson, *The Whole World in His Hands*, 80.
7. Broadcast from Moscow, reprinted in *Paul Robeson Speaks*, 116.
8. Buck, *American Argument*, 126.
9. Interview with Paul Robeson, Jr.
10. Broadcast from Moscow, reprinted in *Paul Robeson Speaks*, 117.

Chapter Eleven

1. Interview by Philip Bolsover, *The London Daily Worker*, 24 November 1937, reprinted in *Paul Robeson Speaks*, 120.

2. Interview with Paul Robeson, Jr.
3. Interview by Julia Dorn, Theatre Arts Committee, July–August 1939, reprinted in *Paul Robeson Speaks*, 130.
4. Ibid., 131.
5. Seton, *Paul Robeson*, 128.
6. As quoted in Edwin P. Hoyt, *Paul Robeson: The American Othello* (Cleveland and New York: World Publishing Co., 1967), 106.
7. Remarks at mass meeting to free Earl Browder, Madison Square Garden, New York, 29 September 1941, reprinted in *Paul Robeson Speaks*, 139–140.

Chapter Twelve

1. Webster, *Don't Put Your Daughter on the Stage*, 107.
2. Interview with Robert Van Gelder, *The New York Times*, 14 January 1944.
3. Webster, *Don't Put Your Daughter on the Stage*, 112.
4. Schlosser, *Paul Robeson: His Career*, 186.
5. Webster, *Don't Put Your Daughter on the Stage*, 107.
6. Schlosser, *Paul Robeson: His Career*, 197.
7. Seton, *Paul Robeson*, 154.
8. Ibid., 155.
9. Webster, *Don't Put Your Daughter on the Stage*, 116.
10. Ibid.
11. Ibid., 117.

Chapter Thirteen

1. Paul Robeson, *Here I Stand*, 29.
2. Remarks to the commissioner of baseball and major league owners, reprinted in *Paul Robeson Speaks*, 152.
3. "Robeson Lauds Russia at Springarn Banquet," *Pittsburgh Courier*, 17 October 1945, reprinted in *Paul Robeson Speaks*, 162.
4. Article by Louis Lautier, *Baltimore Afro-American*, 5 October 1946, reprinted in *Paul Robeson Speaks*, 176.
5. *Report of Joint Fact-Finding Committee on Un-American Activities in California*, on Paul Robeson's appearance on 7 October 1946, published 1947, 289.
6. Seton, *Paul Robeson*, 169.

7. Ibid., 177.
8. "Robeson in Honolulu," *Honolulu Star-Bulletin*, 22 March 1948, reprinted in *Paul Robeson Speaks*, 183.
9. Gilliam, *Paul Robeson: All-American*, 133.
10. Correspondence with Pete Seeger in response to author's questions.
11. Gilliam, 134.

Chapter Fourteen

1. Address at Welcome Home Rally, Rockland Palace, New York City, reprinted in *Paul Robeson Speaks*, 205.
2. Article on Paris Peace Congress, *New York Times*, 21 April 1949.
3. Seton, *Paul Robeson*, 205.
4. Address at Welcome Home Rally, reprinted in *Paul Robeson Speaks*, 209.
5. Ibid., 210.
6. Article on Manning Johnson, *The New York Times*, 15 July 1949.
7. Carl Rowan with Jackie Robinson, *Wait Till Next Year: The Story of Jackie Robinson* (New York: Random House, 1960), 209.
8. Victor S. Navasky, *Naming Names* (New York: Viking, 1980), 190.

Chapter Fifteen

1. Howard Fast, *Peekskill USA* (New York: Civil Rights Congress, 1951), 29.
2. Ibid., 36.
3. Ibid., 65.
4. David King Dunaway, *How Can I Keep From Singing: Pete Seeger* (New York: McGraw Hill, 1981), 19.
5. Fast, *Peekskill USA*, 83.
6. Ibid., 89.
7. Ibid., 123.
8. Ibid., 124.

Chapter Sixteen

1. Notes to article on Robeson testimony, *Paul Robeson Speaks*, 546.

2. Speech delivered at meeting of National Labor Conference for Negro Rights, Chicago, 10 June 1950, reprinted in *Paul Robeson Speaks*, 250.
3. House Committee on Un-American Activities, *Investigation of the Unauthorized Use of United States Passports*, pt. 3, 84th Cong., 2d sess., 12 June 1956, 4494.
4. Paul Robeson, "On Winning the Stalin Peace Prize," *Freedom*, January 1953.
5. Navasky, *Naming Names*, 193.
6. House Committee on Un-American Activities, *Investigation of the Unauthorized Use of United States Passports*, 4494.
7. Ibid., 4495.
8. Ibid., 4504.
9. Ibid., 4506.
10. Ibid., 4506.
11. Statement to press on 14 July 1956, as quoted in *Paul Robeson Speaks*, 436.
12. Interview with Paul Robeson, Jr.

Chapter Seventeen

1. Schlosser, *Paul Robeson: His Career*, 380.
2. Paul Robeson, *Here I Stand*, xi.
3. Author's correspondence with Pete Seeger.
4. Robinson, *Black on Red*, 318.
5. Ibid., 319.
6. Author's correspondence with Howard Fast.
7. Interview with Paul Robeson, Jr.
8. Excerpts from welcome home meeting speech, reprinted in *Paul Robeson Speaks*, 479.
9. Ibid., 480.
10. Message to "Salute to Paul Robeson," Carnegie Hall, New York City, 15 April 1973, reprinted in *Paul Robeson Speaks*, 482.
11. Susan Robeson, *The Whole World in His Hands*, 237.

Bibliography

Books

Adams, Samuel Hopkins. *Alexander Woollcott: His Life and His World*. New York: Reynal and Hitchcock, 1945.

Broun, Heywood Hale. *Whose Little Boy Are You? A Memoir of the Broun Family*. New York: St. Martin's/Marek, 1983.

Buck, Pearl S., with Eslanda Goode Robeson. *American Argument*. New York: John Day Co., 1949.

Caute, David. *The Great Fear*. New York: Simon and Schuster, 1978.

Duberman, Martin. *Paul Robeson*. New York: Alfred Knopf, 1988.

Du Bois, W. E. B. *The Autobiography of W. E. B. Du Bois*. New York: International Publishers, 1968.

Dunaway, David King. *How Can I Keep From Singing: Pete Seeger*. New York: McGraw-Hill, 1981.

Eastman, Max. *Love and Revolution*. New York: Random House, 1964.

Gaines, James R. *Wit's End: Days and Nights of the Algonquin Round Table*. New York: Harcourt Brace Jovanovich, 1977.

Gelb, Arthur, and Barbara Gelb. *O'Neill*. New York: Harper and Brothers, 1962.

Gilliam, Dorothy Butler. *Paul Robeson All-American*. Washington, D.C.: The New Republic Book Co., 1976.

Hoyt, Edwin P. *Paul Robeson: The American Othello*. New York: World Publishing Co., 1967.

Hamilton, Virginia. *Paul Robeson: The Life and Times of a Free Black Man*. New York: Harper & Row, 1974.

Hardwicke, Cedric, as told to James Brough. *A Victorian in Orbit*. London: Methuen & Co., 1961.

Hough, Richard. *Mountbatten*. New York: Random House, 1981.

Mapp, Edward. *Blacks in American Films*. Metuchen, New Jersey: Scarecrow Press, 1972.

Navasky, Victor S. *Naming Names*. New York: Viking, 1980.

The Negro Since Emancipation. Edited by Harvey Wish. New Jersey: Prentice-Hall, 1964.

Poitier, Sidney. *This Life*. New York: Knopf, 1980.

Robeson, Eslanda Goode. *African Journey*. New York: John Day Co., 1945.

_____. *Paul Robeson, Negro*. New York: Harper & Brothers, 1930.

Robeson, Paul. *Here I Stand*. Boston: Beacon Press, 1971, reprint of 1958 edition.

Robeson, Susan. *The Whole World in His Hands: A Pictorial Biography of Paul Robeson*. New Jersey: Citadel Press, 1981.

Robinson, Robert, with Jonathan Slevin. *Black on Red: My 44 Years Inside the Soviet Union*. Washington, D.C.: Acropolis Books, 1988.

Rosenberg, Marvin. *The Masks of Othello*. Berkeley, California: University of California Press, 1961.

Rowan, Carl T., with Jackie Robinson. *Wait Till Next Year: The Story of Jackie Robinson*. New York: Random House, 1960.

Scales, Junius. *Cause at Heart: A Former Communist Remembers*. Athens, Georgia: University of Georgia Press, 1987.

Seton, Marie. *Paul Robeson*. London: Dennis Dobson, 1958.

Sheaffer, Louis. *O'Neill: Son and Artist*. Boston: Little, Brown & Co., 1973.

Webster, Margaret. *Don't Put Your Daughter on the Stage*. New York: Knopf, 1972.

Woollcott, Alexander. *While Rome Burns*. New York: Viking Press, 1934.

Ziegler, Philip. *Mountbatten*. New York: Knopf, 1985.

Unpublished Dissertation

Schlosser, Anatol I. *Paul Robeson: His Career in the Theatre, in Motion Pictures and on the Concert Stage*. New York University, 1970.

Magazine and Newspaper Articles

Miers, Earl Schenck. "Paul Robeson—Made in America." *Nation.* 27 May 1950.
"Paul Robeson, The Great Forerunner." *Freedomways.* 1985.
Thomas, Ron. "NFL's Only Black Coach." *San Francisco Chronicle.* 27 January 1988.
Van Gelder, Robert. Interview with Paul Robeson. *New York Times.* 14 January 1944.

Government Documents

California Legislature. Tenney Committee. *Report of Joint Fact-Finding Committee on Un-American Activities in California.* 1947.
U.S. Congress. House Committee on Un-American Activities. *Investigation of the Unauthorized Use of United States Passports,* pt. 3. 84th Cong., 2d sess., 12 June 1956.

Interviews and Correspondence

Fast, Howard. Letter in answer to author's questions.
Robeson, Paul, Jr. Interview with author.
Robinson, Robert. Interview with author.
Seeger, Pete. Letter in answer to author's questions.

Index